THE STANDARD IS GLORY

Yisrael Ben Avraham

Copyright © 2015 by Yisrael Ben Avraham

The Standard is Glory
by Yisrael Ben Avraham

Printed in the United States of America.

Editing and proofing:
www.christianeditingservices.org

ISBN 9781498447034

All rights reserved solely by the author. The author guarantees all contents are original and do not infringe upon the legal rights of any other person or work. No part of this book may be reproduced in any form without the permission of the author. The views expressed in this book are not necessarily those of the publisher.

Unless otherwise indicated, Scripture quotations taken from the New American Standard Bible (NASB). Copyright © 1960, 1962, 1963, 1968, 1971, 1972, 1973, 1975, 1977, 1995 by The Lockman Foundation. Used by permission. All rights reserved.

Scripture quotations taken from the Amplified Bible (AMP). Copyright © 1954, 1958, 1962, 1964, 1965, 1987 by The Lockman Foundation. Used by permission. All rights reserved.

Scripture quotations taken from the Complete Jewish Bible. Copyright © 1998 by David H. Stern. All rights reserved.

www.xulonpress.com

"A man with an experience is not at the mercy of a man with an opinion."

Pastor L. H. Hardwick

To the eternal sons of glory everywhere abiding
in the perfecting will of the Holy One...
Blessed be He

Content

Acknowledgements vii
Foreward ix
Preface xiii
Introduction xxiii

Chapter 1	First Things First 37
Chapter 2	The Soul 69
Chapter 3	Glory and the Regenerated Spirit 107
Chapter 4	Control—Alt—Delete: The Renewed Mind 132
Chapter 5	Dying to Live – The Living Sacrifice .. 152
Chapter 6	We His People 173
Chapter 7	Live the Experience 189

Acknowledgments

In the space of time I have experienced unspeakable blessings from friends and godly advisors. For these extraordinary people of great faith I bless Adonai. This book carries the Lord's wisdom I have received over the years through many vessels of love. I am grateful to "Ema Paula," a quiet smile with loud love. The years of walking and growing with you have truly been "the way of the heart."

Thank you Doris for your team of professionals as you guys gently edited this work. Patience is clearly demonstrated as your virtue. I am also thankful to Dr. Sharon R. Nesbitt for the new friendship with Sarah and me; we appreciate the Lord's future work with you. May the Lord continue to give you His best and highest.

I am also thankful to those who have helped me in my journey of spirit – to my teacher and friend Eli Ben Yosef in Jerusalem Israel, Jim and Faith Chosa, Saul and Tabitha Avila, Christopher and Dr. Pamela Hardy and my son and daughter Yosef & Rut Avraham; yours is truly a life for a life. I appreciate each one of you and all that have imparted through your uncompromising integrity. To Chavah thank you for allowing the Lord's administrative gift to remain executively excellent. You move at the speed of light, do not stop. Ms. Kim thanks to you I have learned that the simple things are the kindest and that they do matter. Your humility is the Lord's crowning glory upon you.

Most of all I am grateful to my best friend – my beautiful bride Sarah. Your support, prayer and steadfastness are always abounding. You are truly a person of immeasurable compassion and ability.

May this work be for ADONAI and His Eternal glory. You who create unity in the heavens, may You establish shalom throughout Your creation.

Foreword

> *"Now if their fall is riches for the world, and their failure riches for the Gentiles, how much more their fullness! For if their being cast away is the reconciling of the world, what will their acceptance be but life from the dead?*
> **Romans 11:12, 15**

Our understanding of Word, as gentile believers in Jesus Christ, has been limited as a result of several factors. First, the cutting off of the Jewish roots of our faith; a process that began with the Nicene Council in 325 C.E. Second our modern secular thinking and mindset are built on the foundations of Greek thought and philosophy, not the Hebraic mind of Scripture. With the invention of unbiblical replacement theology, by Christian humanist theologians, the cut off became complete. This chasm has not been bridged even when gentile believers in Christ, examine the erudite writings of Ramban, Heschel or Telushkin. These writings find no spiritual resonance. Rabbinic Judaism, absent the Temple and sacrifices, developed to become a faith in works and not the just shall live by faith in Yeshua, the righteousness of God apart from the Torah.

We are the first generation to witness Gentile believers in Christ returning to the Jewish branch and roots of our faith at a time also of the emergence of Jewish believers in Yeshua HaMassiach, who are beginning to publish their works for the One New Man. Jewish believers in Christ bring a new depth and fullness to our understanding of the Word, as they reconnect the New Covenant to its Hebraic foundations, both in language, thought and mindset.

Yisrael's The Standard is Glory paints a canvass of both broad strokes and intricate detail. The broad strokes are to connect God's redemption plan and purpose to the foundational and deep truth of **Romans 11:36**: *"For from Him and through Him and to Him are all things. To Him be the glory forever. Amen"* and **Ephesians 1:10** *"that in the dispensation of the fullness of the times He might gather together in one all things in Christ, both which are in heaven and which are on earth-in Him"*. To these broad strokes, he works to flesh out the details and connect the Glory of the Lord with the 3 seminal elements of Jesus' High Priestly prayer in *John 17*: glory, authority and eternal life.

He explains how the glory of the Lord worked in original creation and in God's salvation plan through Jesus. To the first question the Lord put to fallen Adam and Eve: Where are you? the Lord's salvation plan is to enable us to respond: "I am in Christ." To the question "Who am I?" we are enabled through

Christ to respond, "I am a son/daughter of the Most High!." To the question what is our redeemed life's purpose, we are enabled to respond: " to accomplish the will of Our Father in Heaven."

A principal illustration of our limited understanding is to be found in how we think about salvation. Our focus has been on personal salvation without grasping the full implications and its connection to the Lord's *"restoration of all things."* We have not hitherto understood the fullness of the eternal plan and purpose of the Lord summarized in **Romans 11:36** and **Colossians 1:15-18**, to manifest His Glory in all things. As we come to a fuller understanding of the Lord's manifestation of His Glory in the restoration of all things, we come to a clearer understanding of who we are in Christ and how we are to walk in obedience in order to manifest His glory and accomplish His eternal plan.

We await the manifestation of the *John 17* generation for whom our Lord prayed, which is the **Romans 8:19-25**; a generation of the revelation of the sons of God for which all creation eagerly waits.

We ordinarily have a very limited view of salvation and confine it to personal salvation. Yisrael elevates our understanding to a far greater depth: that the Lord is redeeming not just us, but all creation that belongs to Him. Further that our personal salvation is one of the means through which God reveals His glory. Yisrael repeatedly points to this core understanding that salvation is being joined to the image of the Lord which brings fresh understanding of and that our life's journey from glory to glory is the unfolding of His glory in us. Yisrael brings light to our understanding of likeness and image by deconstructing the Hebrew letters which constitute these central truths of man created in God's likeness and image and connects them to original creation when God breathed into Adam, the cross when Jesus breathed his last breath, to the disciples upon whom Jesus breathed the Holy Spirit after His resurrection and our being born again by water and by the Spirit.

The key is living in obedience to the Father's will. In so doing, the Lord's glory will be revealed in us and we understand what Yeshua meant when He taught that the kingdom of God is within you. Yisrael sharpens our understanding of obedience and its connection to being a living sacrifice and in turn to worship.

It is in the nature of Yisrael's teaching and writing that they bear close and repeated study as he unfolds many layers of the revelation of the Word through its Hebrew text, context and mindset. This does not come easy, as we need to keep the helicopter view as we dive down to the detail. But it is well worth the effort. Writers like Yisrael, help us to plumb the depths and join Paul in marveling: *"Oh the depth of the riches both of the wisdom and knowledge of God!" How unsearchable are His judgments and His ways past finding out!* **Romans 11:33**, *And then to affirm, "For of Him and through Him and to Him are all things, to whom be glory forever. Amen."* **Romans 11:36**

Dr Philip Pillai
Singapore
11 August 2015

Preface

> He asked life of You, You gave it to him, Length of days forever and ever. His glory is great through Your salvation, Splendor and majesty You place upon him. For You make him most blessed forever; You make him joyful with gladness in Your presence.
> *Psalm 21:4-6*

Life is truly a wonderful opportunity given to every person in the world. Salvation in Yeshua is life's true existence given to all who are born again. I write this book for believers; however there is something for anyone reading it. People in general are seekers. It is what they seek and why they are seeking that matters. For the sake of this book, I want to examine the glory of salvation. Yeshua is the King of Glory, but what is this glory that is ruled by His kingship? If there is a king, and if there is glory, then what is it and where is it? The majesty of Messiah is more than a personal salvation. So often believers live far below the Lord's standard of glory.

Many fail to realize what is gained from the resurrection of Yeshua. There is an uncompromising stateliness in the salvation received through Yeshua.

Being born again is the regeneration of the spirit man. Spiritual regeneration births a glorious standard once true salvation finds its proper place within the heart of a person. Yeshua came to give life and that life more abundantly. But what is this abundant life and why is it not in full operation in the life of many believers today? Most Christians spend far too much time seeking the blessings of the Lord from Yeshua's pain on the cross. Salvation is not a personal gain but a kingdom expansion. I have heard many people say, "Yeshua is my personal Savior." This is not true. Yeshua is not a personal "celestial bell hop" that carries the baggage of a person's past. It is not good to think His Lordship is so that our needs might be met based on our personal desires and hopes. What is personal about salvation is our commitment to becoming the new creation in Yeshua.

When believers come to realize that their salvation is an expression of the Lord's will and glory, then they are able to know how salvation testifies. The testimony of Yeshua must still speak today in the lives of those confessing His name. Their witness is for the Lord's kingdom in order to reveal His glory. Believers are to live according to the Lord's will, for His sake, not theirs.

Preface

> You search the Scriptures because you think that in them you have eternal life; it is these that testify about Me; and you are unwilling to come to Me so that you may have life. I do not receive glory from men; but I know you, that you do not have the love of God in yourselves. I have come in My Father's name, and you do not receive Me; if another comes in his own name, you will receive him. How can you believe, when you receive glory from one another and you do not seek the glory that is from the one and only God? *John 5:39-44*

Glory is missed when we live out salvation according to our thoughts and out of our ways. Glory is a now-reality. This now-reality is the constancy of God for now is His salvation! All creation is to be filled with the glory of the Lord: therefore the Lord's glory in all His excellence and brilliance must begin within those called by His name. All that the Lord delights in is in the goodness of His glory. Goodness is absolute and complete. In the Lord's goodness, glory is restoration of the soul. Psalm 23:3 says: "He restores my soul; He guides me in the paths of righteousness For His name's sake." The path of righteousness leads a person into the Lord's goodness by His loving kindness and this is salvation.

Salvation is the existence of the Lord's glory within a person. Being born again is to regain the reality of glory through the Lord's indwelling Spirit. The Hebrew word, "shekinah", connects to the glory of the Lord's presence. God desires to "shekan" or dwell in His creation and, more specifically, His agent *"man-king."* I call humanity *"man-king"* because man as male and female were created to rule over creation according to the Creator's will. To dwell is to lodge, as a verb. Shekinah is the "dwelling of God" or the aspect of God which takes up residence and dwells.

The tabernacle of Moses in the book of Exodus is a good example of a place where the "Shekinah" "shekans" or dwells. Likewise the tabernacle is now the body of the Messiah through the community of believers. But what does it mean to be the Lord's dwelling place? Dwelling is not just a visitation but also an inhabitation. Mistakenly, believers lose the focus of salvation with all sorts of well-intended plans. I have heard both clergy and laity say, "We are here to serve the people." But this is not heaven's perspective. The Lord's will is not for us to serve people. The will of the Lord is always to serve our Father, the Creator of all. And the ultimate example of this is Yeshua.

There comes a point in every person's life when a deep examination of the heart must occur, according to the Lord's rule. It is the time where motives and agendas must be exposed in order to bring order. When the Lord's holiness appears in our lives, it is gentle and kind, yet it exposes the darkness that can exist within the heart. Unless we are walking at the Lord's standard, we still come short of His glory. Salvation touches us to bring about a transformation. When the Lord touches us, He is saying it is time to get on course: your time of corruption is over.

By the Lord's grace and love, I have come to realize how I had overlooked eternal life as something to be experienced now. I lived well below the Lord's standard of glory which caused me to unknowingly dishonor my own destiny and in doing so to dishonor God. I wrote this book with much weeping while I was in Israel. The more I allowed the Lord to quiet my spirit, the more I saw the Lord's grace and how I was to live as a son. Without realizing it, I had made the unimportant important and, in doing so, I had missed the greatest aspect of salvation – the glory.

The human mind perceives through the faculties of intellect and reason. People, for the most part, have more understanding and very little knowing. It is important that knowing is first and understanding is made subject to knowing when it comes to glory. Human nature thinks that when you understand, then you know. Many believe that because they understand something, they know it. But we are to know first and through knowing, understanding comes. When it comes to glory, understanding must be subordinate to knowing. Understanding from unredeemed human insight or ability is a post-fallen condition.

Being created in God's image after His likeness causes a knowing, because we existed before there was a natural "birthday". Understanding must serve knowing because knowing is where man first began in the Lord. Our natural knowing is only understanding facilitated through intellect. Intellect is comprehension. Comprehension is the function of perception. Perception is the insight gained from an experience. I mentioned intellect and reason before because these equate to understanding. The downside to this is that understanding can become idolatry from heaven's point of view when there is no renewed mind.

In Jewish culture, the sages teach that there are two things that are essential to serving God. First, one should accept the yoke of the reign of heaven. Second, one should accept the yoke of God's precepts – this includes the full counsel of God's Word. What I found in my life is that, though I was running the Lord's race, I was not running it with His end in sight. How could I, when I was so far removed from the reality of the beginning of all things? I had head understanding and heart consideration. Though I was a student of God's Word, my heart and life reflected something lesser than the glory of my studies within the gift of salvation.

Teaching people the Bible is not a guarantee of fulfilling the Lord's will. I say "fulfilling His will" because that is what salvation is all about. A person can run with zeal for years but if the zeal comes without experiencing the Father's love, then life becomes nothing more than religious works of self-rightness. It was in such a place that I found myself, which is why I wrote this book. I was not living in the abundant salvation available. Understanding had caused me to partially forfeit my spiritual quest of returning to where all was first created. I came to know that if I was to administrate the Lord's government on the earth, I had to engage glory. I realized that I had not truly taken on the yoke of heaven when I received salvation. I had only a set of rules or instructions, but I lacked the reign of glory. I had received the yoke of the Lord's precepts, but missed the mark of glory.

The yoke mentioned in my previous statement about the sages is similar to the yoke that Yeshua speaks of in Matthew 11:28-30.

> "Come to me, all of you who are struggling and burdened, and I will give you rest. Take my yoke upon you and learn from me, because I am gentle and humble in heart, and you will find rest for your souls. For my yoke is easy, and my burden is light." *(CJB)*

Submission is clearly necessary for God's reign and the acceptance of His word must be in a manner and condition of a "yoke". Glory is directly connected to taking on the yoke of heaven. A yoke involves obedience. Obedience needs no intellectual explanation, but only an acknowledgment of God's will. All intellectual reasoning is immaterial when it comes to surrendering to the Lord. Submission is meaningful only when it is above all reason of mind. To take on the yoke of salvation is to take on the "rulership" of heaven.

Accepting the lordship and kingship of heaven comes through the glorified Messiah, Yeshua, but it does not stop there. God's Word is eternal and never passes away; and if eternal, then time does not affect it in any way—past, present or future. When we accept the lordship and kingship of salvation, we live in the reality of what is eternal. My hope is for the eternal to become your reality. Not as some mystical "spookie" experience, conjured up through deep thought or meditation, but as the Lord reaching out with His love for you.

ADONAI desires the return of what He created – EVERYTHING! Nothing is outside of His will. Nothing is beyond His reach. All things are to work for good through the love our Father and Creator has for all creation, not just mankind. The Lord's standard is glory. It is where all things began and it is where all things will return. When every born-again person reaches the end of self, what remains is truth. Truth is the only way for life eternal to exist. When the Lord's truth comes in contact with a person's spirit and soul, then the reality of Yeshua's glorious body is revealed. As believers reading this, it is important to remember our place in the Lord and that our purpose is to do His will. For someone reading without faith in the Messiah, my hope is that this book becomes the invitation to return to where all things began through the Lord's glorious salvation.

As life eternal becomes the reality of salvation, so does living our life in holiness. Holiness is more than a separation unto the Lord. It is a reverential fear. This fear is not anxiety or apprehension; but it is filled with assurance and ability. We have the Blessed Holy One Himself and our Father's love— a love that causes truth to be made known. In the experience of knowing, we live according to the Lord's standard of glory. Glory was, is and will always remain the standard of the Lord's kingdom and of living with integrity and love.

> Truth is the light that helps you leave the darkness. Turn it on. *Reb Nachman of Breslov*

In the beginning was the Word, and the Word was with God, and the Word was God. He was with God in the beginning. All things came to be through him, and without him nothing made had being. In him was life, and the life was the light of mankind.

John 1:1-4
Complete Jewish Bible (CJB)

Introduction

Jesus spoke these things; and lifting up His eyes to heaven, He said, "Father, the hour has come; glorify Your Son, that the Son may glorify You, even as You gave Him authority over all flesh, that to all whom You have given Him, He may give eternal life. This is eternal life, that they may know You, the only true God, and Jesus Christ whom You have sent. I glorified You on the earth, having accomplished the work which You have given Me to do. Now, Father, glorify Me together with Yourself, with the glory which I had with You before the world was. *John 17:1-5*

In a world where ambition and success are driven by social media networks intimate face-to-face encounters is a lost art. Technology has made life faster but has slowed down heart-felt sincerity. Modern life can be artificial in some ways. Friendships are not what they used to be. A handshake and an eye-to-eye deal is a thing of the past. Yea is no longer yea and nay is no longer nay. Many people are out of touch with most things that do not need to be charged to work: the simple dirt and marbles kind of stuff. At the risk of sounding nostalgic, there was a time when men wore hats and women wore gloves. Principle and purity were partners that served society with joy. Honor was celebrated without compromise. A person's character was devoted to the greater good of all mankind, with a tangible reverence. Living was glorious. Life reflected glory.

I would venture to imagine the apprehension of Yeshua as He was praying during His last moments on earth. He knew His entire existence was for the purpose of being the required sacrifice in all of creation for the debt of sin. It is interesting that Yeshua speaks of things that carry such hope and light at such a dark hour. In His prayer, Yeshua mentions three things concerning His impending death:

1. Glory
2. Authority
3. Eternal life

Who thinks of glory, authority and eternal life at the time of death? What is Yeshua speaking of and why is He speaking in this manner? We know there is nothing inconsequential whenever Yeshua speaks. Though it is near the end of His earthly life mission, His prayer gives insight to the beginning of all life. According to His prayer, the disciples of Yeshua are to know eternal life; but what is this eternal life? Knowing is important to life eternal because it causes a restoration of glory which brings authority. Eternal life is to know the one true God, and to know His sent one, Yeshua the Messiah. In knowing, there is the experience of what was in the beginning, before the world was. Salvation is more than just believing in someone. Salvation is the way restoration takes place for all creation.

The Creator of all things has always been intimately interested in the things concerning man and creation. From Adam to Noah and from Noah until now, the Lord has had only one desire: that is to have His creation restored to what it was when it was first created in all its glory and honor. This may be impossible to believe but nothing is impossible within the framework of salvation. Believers must be disciples that live beyond trusting and believing in the natural. Disciples of Yeshua are required to know and experience the supernatural in light of Yeshua's prayer. I am not referring to a spiritual "twilight zone." I mean living in the reality of a present tense salvation, where life eternal brings the Lord's standard of glory in, where His authority is shifting and changing every dimension of a person's being. Here the Lord's will is clearly revealed to His sons on the earth and creation aligns itself in response.

God's Word records a history that demonstrates eternity engaging time. From Genesis to Malachi and from Matthew to Revelation, the Father wanted something special with His covenanted people, Israel, and the believers in Yeshua. There is a practical exercise I use to help people understand what I am saying. I would ask you to get your Bible in hand now. In your left hand hold Genesis, chapters one and two; and in your right hand hold Genesis 3 to Revelations 22. Now, with these in hand, I want you to see such wonderful love that has never been recorded elsewhere. In Genesis, chapters one and two, is the recorded beginning of creation. From Genesis, chapter three all the way to the back of the book is what the Lord did to return all creation back to Genesis One and Two. Is this not amazing?

As simple as the exercise is, there is actually a great denial among believers that life eternal is something to know now. The straightforward message in the Bible begins and ends with one question that has never changed. It is the same question asked of Adam (male and female). In Genesis 3:9 the Lord calls out, "Where are you?" Adam and Eve never answered this question. An assault of shame, blame and excuses were the repertoire in that unfaithful moment. Though Adam (male/female) had a mouthful of words, it left them empty of what to say.

In the book of Jeremiah the Lord says to Jeremiah: "Before I formed you in the womb I knew you." (Jeremiah 1:5) Every soul has this same intimate beginning with God. God's thoughts toward us bring forth His plan, which results in glory. Before sin-nature and death, man (male and female) walked with God as an image of Him and made in His likeness. ==Man is created by God to reflect His glory.== Mankind was and remains "man-king" as the crown of creation prior to the introduction of sin. While the world has constantly changed throughout history, the Creator has never changed. God's ultimate desire still remains: that His presence be reflected in His male and female persons, made in His image and after His likeness. I want to stop here to make a disclaimer that will be a rule throughout this book. When I refer to "man" or "Adam", I am speaking of both male and female. "God created man in His own image, in the image of God He created him; male and female He created them." (Genesis 1:27) It is necessary to keep this in mind when reading this book.

Salvation is the ultimate revelation of covenant between God and creation. Salvation is about revealing the Lord's glory. A loving and caring Father demonstrates it through His begotten son. As the redeemed of the Lord, believers are children of something greater. Believers in Yeshua are more than what this world thinks. Believers are not to live according to the world's systems but according to the revealing of the Father's kingdom: as sons. I would like to pose a question now. Do you believe heaven is full of Christians or sons of God? Romans 8:14-17 states: "For all who are being led by the Spirit of God, these are sons of God. For you have not received a spirit of slavery leading to fear again, but you have received a spirit of adoption as sons by which we cry out, 'Abba! Father!' The Spirit Himself testifies with our spirit that we are children of God, and if children, heirs also, heirs of God and fellow heirs with Christ, if indeed we suffer with Him so that we may also be glorified with Him." God is looking for obedient sons to fulfill His will in the earth. Eternal life through the Messiah is the reclamation of an honored position that reflects the manifold truth of the Father's faithfulness in man.

Man is the image of God's seal on creation. It has been said that God has no physical image, but this is not necessarily accurate. Colossians 1:15 says Yeshua is the "image of the invisible God, firstborn of all creation." Salvation is the image of God. As believers in salvation, our born-again life is the image of the Creator. This image expresses the Father's will, which in turn is His seal.

In Hebraic thought, a seal represents truth. *Emet* is the Hebrew word for truth. Truth, in the Hebrew language, has a concrete definition. Truth, in most cases, is set against its counterpart "lie" and is typically dominant in thought; however, this conclusion is incorrect when relating to truth and God. Truth is the function of God's intention. It is the substance that causes all things to be. There is a chapter in my book, *Kingdom Armor,* that explains truth in more detail. But for now, truth is the substance of God's design and intention. In simple terminology, redeemed man is the substance of what has never changed in God. When Adam disobeyed the Lord's instructions in Genesis 3, it changed man, not the Creator of man.

What happened in the Garden of Genesis with male and female still occurs every day. The act of making choices

Introduction

within the framework of "self" still remains the cause of all that opposes God's will. What took man from the presence of God continues to take him now. It is because of disobedience that salvation needed to exist. It is because of obedience that salvation does exist. It is only the will of the Father, specified in Yeshua's prayer in John 17, that is important. The Lord's kingdom is centered on this one thing: the Father's will. Salvation is the pathway to what has never changed in God. Looking into Scripture, in both the former and renewed covenant, the Hebrew-Christian faith expresses its hope in terms of the kingdom of God. The Lord's kingdom is immovable and is always abounding, yet it requires what many fail to fully live—obedience. Obedience is man's standard whereby the Lord's glory is revealed. When the Lord's glory is revealed so is man's dignity. This is the kingdom.

The kingdom of God is about that steadfast conversation between a son and his Father. True relationships in life must be established by unconditional love. "For God so loved the world that He gave His only begotten Son, that whoever believes in Him shall not perish, but have eternal life." (John 3:16) The light of a present tense salvation must be the Father's love. The reality of this is to believe in God's love, which makes us His sons.

All of creation is purposed and loved by the Creator, not just man. The greatest demonstration of love is in the act of giving. The Lord gave us His unconditional love which establishes salvation. Iniquity, sin and transgression caused man to enter into a condition where God's glory could no longer reside. These conditions changed the relationship between Creator and creation. It is imperative to acknowledge that disobedience changed everything.

It is God's unconditional love that brings the restoration of life eternal for the glory of God. There are so many believers today that have no idea or experience of God's unconditional love. He is love and there is never a time or condition where He does not love what He created. God always moves according to His desire and His desire is for all to return to Him. A modern description of God's love might include His power and the glory of His Church. The church I am speaking of is governmental. The government was laid upon the shoulders of Yeshua. The High Priest of Israel also carried the government upon His shoulders when he bore the names of the sons of Israel.

The administration and the executing power of God's kingdom govern the things of God. The kingdom of God is the place where all things come. All things came from within the Holy One Himself. Selah! Ponder on that for a moment. There is nothing that exists that did not exist in God. All things, seen or unseen, exist because of the Creator, our Father, the Eternal One. The kingdom is before the Garden of Eden. The kingdom is from within the Lord. The garden is where separation from the kingdom took place because the corruption of desire caused the function of choice, which introduced sin-nature. We must see and know the Lord's

Introduction

ruling as His reigning. It is eternal, according to the will of Him who causes all things to be. His reign is a position and the realm is the Lord's dwelling.

To go from glory to glory is redemption at different levels, according to the Lord's will. The level of glory is equal to the level at which the Lord wants to reveal Himself. True sons of God are to live going from glory to glory. Many believers, however, live going from story to story, never coming into the Lord's fullness. The full manifestation of God's kingdom comes when the sons of God administer the Father's will. Creation is waiting for sons to manifest so that it is able to submit and come under God's government and order.

Yeshua said, "Beware of the wolves in sheep's clothing." (Matthew 7:15) He goes on to say: "Many will say to Me on that day, 'Lord, Lord.'" (v. 22) But the accounting of salvation is in His concluding statement: "And then I will declare to them, 'I never knew you; depart from Me, you who practice lawlessness.'" (v. 23) What a sobering thought to know that, just because a person follows traditions, customs and culture, he cannot claim to be a son of God. When I read Matthew chapter 7 some years ago, I thought it was not as important that I knew the Lord, but that He knew me. I realized that I could not know the Lord through my limited human abilities. How can the finite ever fully grasp the infinite? And I am using low-level words that do not even fit the magnitude of the Almighty. I quickly began to change my prayer from *Let me know You* to *Father, You know me*. You see, only God knows His will and there is a will and plan for each of us. This is what He wants to bring about. Let us speak: "Lord, You knew me before I was in my mother's womb. Holy Spirit, bring forth what is inside me that has never changed in You and that has always been there in me by our Father's will. Father, as Your son, may You know me in the way I was created by You, through the sonship, lordship and kingship of Yeshua the Messiah. I accept Your Spirit to bring forth Your identity and Your destiny for my life."

At the center of this thought is Yeshua's life, death, burial and resurrection. Traditional salvation, in simple religious terms, is accepting Yeshua as the begotten son of God, according to Romans 10:8-10. Though this theology is the believed norm, it falls terribly short in comparison to the message of biblical repentance. Repentance as seen in the Bible is a message of return. Israel's salvation came by the "saving acts" of the Lord. It is the loving kindness of God that keeps Israel from complete annihilation, a love based on a covenant promise.

As the Body of Messiah, believers are the stewards of kingdom revelation and kingdom manifestation. This can occur only by returning to the standard set by the King of Glory. There must be a hunger for infinite truth. Truth at this level comes with a price and comes from someone greater than ourselves. It is at this level of truth that the standard is raised. To be given the gift of salvation is really the greatest miracle of all and within it is the ultimate truth without end.

Introduction

Outside the culture of those first believers in Yeshua it is virtually impossible to comprehend, much less experience, a higher and deeper level of returning to God in Spirit and in truth.

The early apostles, and all of Israel in the Jewish community within the Roman-ruled world, understood the importance of being subject to God as King and to His kingdom. The first message of the gospel was not the preaching of Yeshua as the Messiah but was the call of returning, or better said, "turning" toward God. Yeshua was the way, but the message was return. John's message when baptizing was *repent*. Yeshua's message was to *repent*. Peter's first message in Acts announces: "Repent!" Yeshua is the way by which man and creation is able to return to their point of origin— God. Salvation, in the kingdom of God, is about returning. Repentance was the message then; and it is the same today.

Yeshua's prayer in John 17 has such a place of honor. The Lord is thinking of me, you and all the world alike. Scripture teaches that all have sinned and fallen short of the glory of God. It is this passage that helps every believer to accept people where they are, while realizing that there is a restored glory coming upon them. Yeshua did not come seeking the lost; the Lord, who is all-knowing, has never lost His creation. He did know where Adam was when He asked, "Where are you?" Yeshua came to seek what was lost: the loving relationship between man and the Father of all creation.

God is the Creator of all things and He knows all things. For the Creator, was something lost that needed to be restored?

God asks Adam, "Where are you?" But what is He asking, really? Man (male and female) had become aware of himself and lost sight of God. A better understanding of God's question is: "Why are you not reflecting the same level of light as Me?" As the image of God, and made after His likeness, all that should be reflected is God in all of His glory. Once man took from what was forbidden (see Genesis 2:15-17), man could only reflect what was now inside him—the knowledge of good and evil.

Yeshua, as the Word made flesh, is the revealing of the Father. The word made flesh reveals what comes from the Holy One Himself. This revelation is light. Light is not something that is seen as a focal point; light makes seeing possible. Another way of knowing this is to ask ourselves, when we walk into a dark room and turn on a light, is it the light we look at or is it what the light reveals in the room? This is why the Lord says in the beginning: "Let there be light." A function of revelation needed to be created in order for creation to be revealed and, in doing so, God could be known.

Salvation restores man's ability to see to the level where God can be reflected. When you have been in a dark place and a light is turned on, it takes a while for the eyes to adjust. This adjusting period can be uncomfortable but something important is happening. Eyes are amazing for human vision because of the incredible range they have. The dark center of the eye, known as the pupil, contracts and expands depending on the amount of light; and it can block the amount of light the eye receives in bright situations. Taking this little bit of information further spiritually, the eyes of Adam were opened when the Father's will was not obeyed. What was forbidden became the light by which man began to see. At a very fundamental level, salvation restores eyesight. Because we see through the mind, will and emotions, all seeing passes through the flesh. Flesh is the perception of what pleases "self". When nakedness appeared, seeing as God sees was lost and thereby glory was lost. In the beginning, man's perception was the way of knowing. With the glorious substance of truth lost, the soul became fragmented.

Salvation means being joined to the image of the Lord. I am going to repeat this because it is important. Salvation is being joined to the image of the Lord. To know salvation is to have the constant experience of the Lord restoring glory. This restoration is the regeneration of man's spirit. Yeshua's resurrection is the power of our life as spirit beings. Remember that being a believer in Yeshua is to also believe in the life of His Spirit. Life is not just overcoming sin and death; life is the birthing of Spirit from eternity. We are not born again from the level of the earth. Yeshua conquered everything associated with that corruption. We are born again from the very breath of the Creator. Once you are born again what is there to believe? The light of the Lord's glorious and eternal kingdom opens the eyes to what has always been.

The Lord is not bringing Himself into us. The Lord is bringing us into Himself. Salvation is redemption. Keep in mind that you are joined to the Lord. Glory is a weighty matter and must be realized beyond ideologies of self-glory. Who we are has nothing to do with what we may or may not possess on the earth. The Lord's standard of glory is the disrobing of earthly accomplishments, and the revealing of what has never changed and what has always been waiting to come forth.

Salvation is the covering that now clothes believers with a holy identity. Yeshua has restored those that believe in him to life eternal. Salvation is now; therefore life eternal is now. Today the Lord poses this question to every person: "Can you love the one I love?" In loving the Lord we discover, through His eyes, that we are eternally loved. Believers are given spiritual identity and an eternal destiny because of such love. All of mankind rested in the loins of Adam; therefore God calls to all humanity in Genesis 3:9. It is in the "where are you" call that we have been given the answer in Yeshua so that we might once again bear the light of glory in the world. The one true calling of the Lord is to live, move and have our being in Him. Messiah's glory is His authority over our lives as servant sons in the Lord's kingdom.

> For Adonai takes delight in his people, he crowns the humble with salvation. *Psalm 149:4 (CJB)*

Chapter 1

First Things First

—▶•◀—

Then God said, "Let Us make man in Our image, according to Our likeness; and let them rule over the fish of the sea and over the birds of the sky and over the cattle and over all the earth, and over every creeping thing that creeps on the earth." God created man in His own image, in the image of God He created him; male and female He created them. *Genesis 1:26-27*

Man is made in the image of God and after His likeness. There are four different Hebrew words that can be translated as image or likeness. For the sake of time, I will only mention the two that relate to the above scripture reference.

Tselem – Genesis 1:26
Derived from "tsal", meaning a shadow. *Tselem* is the outline or shape of a shadow.

Demut – Genesis 1:26
Derived from the Hebrew word "dam" meaning blood. *Demut* is best described as one descended from the "blood" of another and who bears a resemblance to the one descended from.

It is important to keep in mind that Hebrew is a language of function, and therefore of action. The reality of man (male and female) is not the appearance of an image but intention. God placed within man a shadow or representation of His own function—a goal, purpose, thought, etc. As the image of God, all of mankind has the responsibility of living in the same manner as God. The Eternal Creator, as Master of all, filled man with the representation of Himself. Think about that.

Tselem is an outline for the Lord to fill with Himself. Man is like his Creator or as his "shadow" (tselem). So if image is not an appearance, then what is reflected as God after His likeness? It is what acts as He does. What manifests is not so much an appearance but a way of seeing. Image is also having the ability to see how God reveals Himself in us, in order for us to function as He functions. This is why graven images are an abomination to God because they do not do this. When a person worships an idol, they are actually projecting themselves on to the idol. An idol cannot give the ability to function nor see in order to reflect its purpose. Idolatry is man's darkest worship of self.

God also made man after His likeness. Likeness in the Hebrew is "demut". *Demut* gives the function of blood. As mentioned earlier, "demut" comes from the Hebrew word "dam", meaning blood. *Dam* is spelled with two Hebrew letters "dalet" and "mem". *Dalet* functions as a door representing a back-and-forth motion. The second letter, *mem,* represents fluid, which can speak of blood. Looking at *dalet* and *mem* together, we get the notion of flowing blood because it moves back and forth. If we are made in God's likeness, this means that man has been endowed with the ability to move as the Lord moves.

There are some wonderful insights regarding the process of God's creating and making in Genesis 1. "In the image of God He *created* him (man)." (Genesis 1:27), but in Genesis 9:6 it says: "...for in the image of God He *made* man." The verb used in the first context is "created" and it is transliterated from the Hebrew "bara", which denotes creation ex nihilo (i.e., from nothing). But, the verb used in Genesis 9, in the second context, is "asah" or "made", which implies taking something that already exists and perfecting it by making it better. These two verbs appear in the first account of creation to denote different levels of creation. The third verb, "yatsar" or "formed", appears in the second account of creation and serves as a "mediator" between "created" and "made". It implies "making something from something" (i.e., in the second account of creation, man was formed from the dust of the ground.

The reason why these three verbs are important is because there is a clear example of what it means to go from glory to glory. Something from nothing is the first level of creation—*bara*. This is the beginning of expressed glory proceeding from the Creator. The next level of expressed glory is something from something, which is "formation". This is the continuation God expresses of His glory, in His image, after His likeness. The final level of expressed glory is perfecting something that exists—*asah*. This is the action of the Creator's will. Looking at all three, there is the common link of God revealing Himself.

Adam walked in creation at the speed of God revealing Himself. In the beginning, Adam cast no shadow of his own. Man (male and female) as "the place where God fills" is the shadow of God becoming as the former reflects the Father. Adam, as image and likeness, is first blood or first life that is God-like. The image of seeing in the likeness of God is the active expression of glory. Glory is in all that God created: this means that that every aspect of created reality is intended to reflect and reveal the presence of the Creator. Awareness at this level brings the Lord's will into existence, and this is His honor and glory.

Man, in the beginning, walked in the spirit wind of the day. Male and female functioned at the moment where the Lord revealed Himself as a spirit being. Every believer in Yeshua is birthed again into this position. This sounds simple and may not seem important when it comes to daily salvation. But this simple statement is the access point to all that is God and His kingdom. In John 3:3, Yeshua speaks to Nicodemus: "I say to you, unless one is born again he cannot see the kingdom of God." Yeshua also told His disciples, in Luke 18:17: "Truly I say to you, whoever does not receive the kingdom of God like a child will not enter it at all."

The first reality of salvation is the image of the invisible expressed through the begotten son. Once this is truly realized, the image of the invisible continues to be reflected in the person that lives in the light of this revelation. Yeshua, while praying in John 17, first mentions glory. He says to His Father: "Glorify your Son, so that the Son can glorify you." Glory is connected to regeneration. Yeshua is asking His Father to return him to the place he once knew as the only reality for His perfect existence. Now if Yeshua is without sin, then His request is right and true. He legally is in the position to make such a request.

> But as many as received Him, to them He gave the right to become children of God, even to those who believe in His name, who were born, not of blood nor of the will of the flesh nor of the will of man, but of God. And the Word became flesh, and dwelt among us,

and we saw His glory, glory as of the only begotten from the Father, full of grace and truth. *John 1:12-14*

At the time of Yeshua's praying, the fullness of who He was, is and always will be was coming to fulfillment on earth. Yeshua is full of grace. Grace is not "unmerited favor". How could it be when the prince of the world could find nothing in Yeshua. In salvation, grace is power. It is the power that rests upon a person, causing him to be what he was created to be. Glory is honor. Glory is the uprightness and devotion that comes through reverence. Yeshua obeyed His Father's will on earth and it was now time for God to honor His son. In other words, to "glorify" the son.

In being a son, Yeshua had proven who He was in the flesh by overcoming the flesh. He had lived as an example of wholeness that succeeded the Torah (instructions/law). The instructions of God to the children of Israel were never about salvation. The "law" is commonly connected to salvation as works-righteousness. It is important to note here, when speaking of the Torah/law, that Israel was given it as a way to live before God as His chosen people. Israel was already "saved" from Egyptian bondage when the "Law of Moses" was given to them. Miriam, Moses' sister, breaks into a song-and-dance routine in Exodus 15. Israel's "salvation" is before Law. Paul speaks how the law is in place, because it shows another law at work in the members of his body. (See

Romans 7:22-24) The Torah should never have been seen as a way to salvation in its original context. The Torah reveals the weakness of flesh which is caused by another law in the body's members. This law is sin.

Glory is the standard for righteousness in order to live according to the Word of God. Glory has many facets but it always brings honor to God. The glory that comes from true salvation must be put in its proper place first through the regeneration of man's spirit. Our spiritual nature is the fundamental element to life. Being born again is to have a regenerated spirit. This regeneration is the restoration to perceive spiritually. It is by the Spirit of the Lord that spiritual truths can be known and received.

Genesis 1:26-27 lets us know how man is created as the image and likeness of the Almighty Creator. I would stop here to say a person must know this without any reservations. Until this is absolutely settled, there is no going further. It must be established, once and for all, as accepted truth that God is the Creator of all creation and is the Master of man. In this mastery everything is from the Lord's perspective. Nothing outside of this can dictate the reality of what is spiritual and therefore what is eternal life. We cannot know the Lord and His truth from earth's perspective. The original state of mankind was spirit, not flesh. As His image and likeness, the Lord addresses believers as spiritual beings, and this is the "sonship" that is to be reflected in salvation. Anything other than this is error and will lead to the "soulish" bondage of self. Man (male and female) is at his greatest in the original glory, as God's image and likeness. Before the nature of sin, all was the glory of God. All was functioning according to the design of God's will.

Creation is created for the sake of things that are called "beginning". It is what is first. First is not sequential. First is original and essential. All that exists is established because there is a beginning. There is a small hint to experiencing truth at the conclusion of the creation account. Transliterated, the final three letters of the three concluding words in Hebrew, we find "bara Elohim la'asot." This statement is in Genesis 2:3 and translates as "God created to do". The Hebrew letters *aleph – mem -- tav*, spell the word *emet*, the Hebrew word for truth. Truth is God's essential will. Truth is the power to realize the deepest potential and purpose. It is to manifest the ultimate awareness of the Lord's capacity for faithfulness. This is the substance of glory for mankind and all creation.

When Yeshua is received as Lord and King, it is His saving act that becomes His seal. In the beginning, before all things changed, the Lord's will was man's only realization and reality. That is difficult to take in if the spirit is not truly regenerated and the mind is not renewed. Man serves as the external expression of an internal impression—this is image and likeness. It is mind-boggling to think about it. However, when salvation is lived beyond a confession, and a sip of juice and a cracker, the eyes become enlightened and knowing God is made real. We experience God's attributes that are based on this level of truth.

God's voice, in the beginning, was the primary source of man's experience. Man was intimately aware that his existence was within the will of God. The voice of God was the substance of his being. The truth was intended will as pure, divine substance which, at this point, man recognized and knew. The Lord's will as the eternal record of Himself was, and still remains as, man's DNA of the spirit. There is a record of every person in the DNA memory of the Lord. Man, as male and female, existed in truth and not in what is good. Man was aligned in his behavior with the Creator's voice as His will and word.

God's desire is for His truth to prevail so that His will becomes living substance through a person's obedience. The reason why many do not live at this level is because of the corruption of self-desire. We live in a world full of self. It is a world that has determined what is good and what is evil, what is right and what is wrong. People have become gods in their own eyes, which causes them to forget their spiritual identity and eternal destiny already recorded inside. Without divine destiny there is no spiritual experience. Without spiritual experience there is no supernatural restoration of the soul.

After the born-again experience, a person undergoes a sanctification process. It begins with the acknowledgment of being a sinner. A sinner is a person failing to see as the Lord created life to be. It is to no longer have glory as the mark of the Lord. Confession of sin begins the conversation of turning to God. During this conversation comes the recognition of salvation because of the Son. From there, as the Lord reveals Himself to us, we stop sinning or living out of the corrupt nature of self and begin living according to the Father's will. At this level of relationship, as His sons, we cease to have the function of desire. Sinners do not practice sin; they practice what they desire which, in turn, is lawlessness. (see 1 John 3:4) Lawlessness is living out of desire: the seed of self. The body of "self" leans to its own understanding and can never follow the Lord's true directive. A person is not a sinner because of sin. A person is a sinner because of desire. If there is no desire, then there will be no sinful act. It is the corruption of having desire that functions against the Father's will. This is what takes place in the garden in Genesis 3:6.

> "When the woman saw that the tree was good for food, and that it was a delight to the eyes, and that the tree was desirable to make one wise, she took from its fruit and ate."

In Genesis chapter three – three events take place:
1. Man's eyes are opened.
2. Nakedness becomes a known substance for truth.
3. Fear becomes the first gateway of the soul.

Keep in mind that male and female eat only the fruit of the tree of the knowledge of good and evil. Fruit is "peri" in the Hebrew. It means earnings, results, or reward. The root of "peri" is "parah" meaning to bear fruit, increase, make fruitful. At the creation of man in God's image and likeness, mankind is at their highest eternal reality. At the moment of their choice, mankind is at their lowest reality by knowing only good and evil. All that is in the world today is good and evil. An unredeemed person can only operate through knowing good and evil. Taking from the tree of knowing good and evil changed everything. When male and female became aware of their nakedness, vanity appeared. What would vanity be at this point in Adam? Let us keep it simple: vanity is seeing yourself. I think it is interesting that the piece of furniture with a mirror is called a vanity. A mirror reflects what stands in it. Vanity is the greatest stronghold in the world and pride is its personality.

Vanity sees through the eyes of self. Even in doing what is good and right, vanity expresses itself through false behavior, false belief, false value, false identity and false authority. Vanity encourages personal agendas and the motivations of men. Vanity is Satan's greatest stronghold over mankind because of opened eyes. Insecurity exists because of vanity. Vanity is ineffective, insignificant in the kingdom of God. It has no place in the nature of a believer. You can allow the Holy Spirit to work on your character or you can let Satan turn you into a character. The futility of man is the result of disobedience. In the beginning man went from spiritual to flesh; from relationship to religion; from responsive to reactive; from tending to toiling, from steward to slave, from glory to groveling.

Glory is lost to knowing good and evil. Immediately following man's actions, thoughts came through the experience of partaking in both good and evil. The first seed of the unfruitful act of disobedience was the use of fig leaves to cover nakedness. I use the word "seed" because the method of creation is fruit with seed in it. Seed produces fruit with seed. Seed is a conceptual idea as opposed to just a natural kernel. A seed speaks of a continuation of a thing; and in the case of man's act, good and evil are the only functions by which knowing occurs for man. God and glory are no longer the standard.

Good and evil are of the same substance: death. Both are given equal place in God's will as transgression. The Lord says: "The day you eat you shall die." (Genesis 2:7) The will of God had been violated and an illegal seizure of glory occurred. Neither good nor evil is greater or lesser than the other. Before that moment, the Lord was the covering by way of His Eternal record. The Eternal Father had given Adam "male and female" the greatest perfection: and that was their ability to experience and see Him. The Lord had also given them the power of perfection in being His stewards over all creation. The eternal mandate for mankind has never changed.

The Word of God is eternal and, if eternal, then it still stands for those who are in salvation and called by His name.

> God blessed them; and God said to them, "Be fruitful and multiply, and fill the earth, and subdue it; and rule over the fish of the sea and over the birds of the sky and over every living thing that moves on the earth." *Genesis 1:28*

Our eternal directive is to be fruitful, multiply, fill the earth and to subdue it. These four commands are divinely decreed and nothing in creation can stop them. It is only with man's consent that can something other than this could be authorized to rule.

Man's original will is God's will. Man had no free will. I am speaking here of the time before the sin covering. Free will is anything that is not the Father's will. There would be no need to have choice when all that existed was creation according to God's will. Remember, we must recognize that before the sin covering, all things were eternal and indeed still are. Everything changed the moment humanity acted outside of what God intended. Free will is not free. Free will cost man life and light. The tree of the knowledge of good and evil does not give the understanding of right and wrong. It transformed man's comprehension. Good and evil became relevant as part of our consciousness. Only after consuming the fruit did the knowledge of good and evil assimilate into the structure of man's being. God said that when the fruit of good and evil was consumed, man would die. Man conformed into death, and life eternal was no longer available to him. With the eternal life lost, glory no longer has a place to exist. Now let us talk about what the eternal and eternity is.

There are several Hebrew words that speak of eternal and eternity. Eternal is "qedem", which is to mean the front, east or formerly. The Hebrew word for eternity is "olam" meaning "in the far distance". *Olam* is used for time as a distant past or a faraway future. *Olam* is frequently translated as eternity or forever but is misinterpreted to mean a "continual span of time that never ends". In Hebraic thinking *olam* is what is at or beyond the horizon. In Hebrew the expression "l'olam va'ed" translates as "forever and ever" but its distinct meaning is "further than now." Eternity expresses the idea of a very ancient past or very distant future.

I mentioned "horizon" because, when standing on land looking out over water, it appears that the sun is touching the earth. Now to ancient people this was eternity because your field of sight was limited, according to where you were standing. The place where the sun appeared to be touching the earth was called "the place where light gathers". *Olam* is not the endless or the ongoing without end. It is what is beyond what the natural eye can see. As we stand on the seashore, our eyes can see only so far in the direction of the sun as where it appears to be touching earth. This does not mean there is nothing beyond that point. It is only that we are in a certain place, a place which allows us to see only so far. Likewise, man's position in "self", through knowing only good and evil, caused eternity and the eternal things to be where God's light is. Without returning what is revealed in God, there is only darkness that survives.

In original intent, it is safe to say, our souls were in constant and unbroken conversation with the Holy One, full of grace as the substance of truth. In the beginning, being in the image and likeness of God meant to carry spiritual identity and eternal destiny. Adam is a being of life. Adam is a living soul because he is *being* life, not *living* life. Life as we know and understand it did not exist prior to the sin covering of flesh.

The Devil is in the Details

Satan, in the beginning, needed to somehow corrupt man's existence and could only do so by man's willingness. "Man-king" had rule over all creation because of the details of God's character and nature, and because he was made in His image and likeness. The original identity is the record from our Eternal Father. As a being of life, Adam (male and female) had God's spiritual identity. The detail of this identity is God's eternal record. It truly is HIS-STORY. This history goes all the way back to Adam in the Lord.

DNA is hereditary material and is truly the book of life. DNA is memory, which is history. Scientists only discovered

DNA. Scientists did not create DNA. DNA is an abbreviation for deoxyribonucleic acid and is found in every cell in the human body. DNA determines the physical qualities of a person, including hair and eye color, height, bone density and thousands of other features. It is the blueprint for the human body. An essential property of DNA is that it can replicate, or make copies of itself. Each strand of DNA in the double helix can serve as a pattern for duplicating the sequence of base proteins. This is indispensable when cells divide because each new cell needs to have an exact copy of the DNA that was present in the old cell. Stepping back for a moment, let us look at what was just said: *there needs to be an exact copy of something for replication to occur*. Satan cannot create anything, but he can falsely duplicate it through imitation. Satan needed to introduce his rebellious substance into man's being. He needed to twist God's perfect man into an image that would serve him through the body of self. Satan cannot change life but he can change what we know about life, which is true perversion.

Satan approaches the female with a deceiving proposition. Genesis 3:4-5: "The serpent said to the woman, "You surely will not die! For God knows that in the day you eat from it your eyes will be opened, and you will be like God, knowing good and evil." Satan is after the eternal record of the Father that was resting inside "man-king". The serpent says that "you will be like God, knowing good and evil." This subliminal message introduces man's only true religion: the religion of "I".

It is in the "I" where Satan was able to take authority from man. Satan himself wanted to be like God but needed the only legal representative that existed, which was man. The "I" is the body of self where a person worships through the desires of his unredeemed soul. There is nothing more than this—the "I" in self without salvation. How self is displayed differs based on a legal, spiritual position and what has been corrupted by desire. A legal position is what people allow through choice. What we choose will give God His place or Satan his "misplace". I say "misplace" because Satan has no place at all. He is always only misplaced. Man, in his actions, replicates the demonic principle of "I" and begins to carry what is now the twofold good and evil book of life within his human DNA.

It is in this human record that sin nature reproduces after its kind through the familial and the familiar. As long as there are unresolved and unredeemed issues within a bloodline, genetics and genealogy will only reflect the corruption of Satan's plan for man. What is natural in a family is passed down genetically because what is done in the flesh remains. It is by choice things are passed down. Every choice has a cause and affects everything, regardless of how small the effect may be. Whatever is ruling over a life is not there by happenstance. It is there because of what has happened in the history of that family. The history of that family becomes the familiar and this is how family perpetuates Satan's plan for that bloodline. Leviticus 17:11: "For the life of the flesh is in the blood." This is not restricted to animal sacrifice. All flesh carries a life with a history. *Familiar* is an interesting word if you look closely at it. The word "liar" is in the word familiar. Families, for centuries, live by the lie that is recorded in their bloodlines. Every sin gives an opening to Satan and allows him to torment next generations to continue the wrong behavior, personality, character and nature of their ancestors, and none of these are of God.

> And the great dragon was thrown down, the serpent of old who is called the devil and Satan, who deceives the whole world; he was thrown down to the earth, and his angels were thrown down with him. Then I heard a loud voice in heaven, saying, "Now the salvation, and the power, and the kingdom of our God and the authority of His Christ have come, for the accuser of our brethren has been thrown down, he who accuses them before our God day and night. And they overcame him because of the blood of the Lamb and because of the word of their testimony, and they did not love their life even when faced with death. *Revelation 12:9-11*

Satan stands to accuse because he has no redemption. Think about that for a moment. There is no salvation for Satan. Since there is no salvation for him, he will never return to his glorious position. Satan has no redemption, therefore he has no forgiveness. Without forgiveness there is only the accusation of what has been witnessed. There is never a release of a debt. Satan can only function as an accuser and this is his only position against man. When we follow after what we want, we make Satan's testimony valid which, in turn, makes him appear to have power over us. The power is rather in our will, which is given over to him when we fall into a temptation. A temptation is nothing more than a desire that is not God's will. Remove this desire and the power of the enemy is gone. Yeshua destroyed all of this, but it is up to a person to live beyond the death of self through the power of the resurrection. Ask yourself this: "What was resurrected when I became alive in Messiah?" It was not your old nature, that's for sure!

> I have been crucified with Christ; and it is no longer I who live, but Christ lives in me; and the life which I now live in the flesh I live by faith in the Son of God, who loved me and gave Himself up for me. *Galatians 2:20*

The devil is "in the details" because he needs the facts of life. The facts of life for humanity are in our bloodlines. Those details about who we are and where we come from give a record of who and what has been ruling over our households. Salvation reaches into the generations still living inside of us, cleansing and clearing out what has blocked the Lord's record where His glory still exists.

> "Beware of the false prophets, who come to you in sheep's clothing, but inwardly are ravenous wolves. You will know them by their fruits. Grapes are not gathered from thorn bushes nor figs from thistles, are they? So every good tree bears good fruit, but the bad tree bears bad fruit. *Matthew 7:15-17*

A tree is known by its fruit and trees are the fruit of a seed. The fruit of man's choice is the false covering or the religion of "I". It is being "like god" that determines what is good and what is evil. In Ancient Israel, a tree was known by its fruit, not by its trunk or its leaves. Appearances are misleading. Satan was able to change the appearance of creation through man's choice. Note I said the "appearance", not creation itself. It is only when ADONAI spoke in Genesis 3:17 that things were cursed. By outward appearances man has lived with eyes opened to self. The body of self has been formed over the centuries because of the experience of what is good or evil. The character and nature of God's glory began diminishing the moment man began to know good and evil.

Man's disobedience, introduced through deception, changed everything.

Deception is the source of desire, and it began with Satan's deceptive attempt at ascending above the Almighty God. Satan lost his place and wanted everything else to lose its place as well. The utmost deception is to be created and then think oneself to be greater than the Creator. Satan is a created being and nothing more. It is clear why Satan himself is the deceiver. He is deceived by what he thought was the source of power: his nature and what he was created to be. Deception is key for the enemy to succeed since Satan cannot create anything. He can only imitate what he has and this is what he uses against mankind. Deception is not power but the skill of persuasion. When a person is deceived, they are under the influence of the deceiver. Satan deceives people through what they desire. The power of the enemy is only in believing his lies.

Yeshua gives insight to the language of the devil in John 8:44: "You are of your father the devil, and you want to do the desires of your father. He was a murderer from the beginning, and does not stand in the truth because there is no truth in him. Whenever he speaks a lie, he speaks from his own nature, for he is a liar and the father of lies." The language of the enemy is recorded as lies within our human DNA. But who created our DNA after all? The Lord God Almighty did! Bless the Lord, oh my soul, we are not stuck to remain the way we are! There is an eternal record to live out of that goes all the way back to Adam and then back into eternity. The Lord wants to reveal His glory from the eternal record that stands from within Himself. Glory has a record of every person. It is this record that is the true standard of life for each and every person.

The Son is in Salvation

> So there are three witnesses *in heaven: the Father, the Word and the Holy Spirit, and these three are One; and there are three witnesses on the earth*: the Spirit, the water, and the blood; and these three agree [are in unison; their testimony coincides]. If we accept [as we do] the testimony of men [if we are willing to take human authority], the testimony of God is greater (of stronger authority), for this is the testimony of God, even the witness which He has borne regarding His Son. He who believes in the Son of God [who adheres to, trusts in, and relies on Him] has the testimony [possesses this divine attestation] within himself. He who does not believe God [in this way] has made Him out to be *and* represented Him as a liar, because he has not believed (put his faith in, adhered to, and relied on) the evidence (the testimony) that God has borne regarding His

Son. And this is that testimony (that evidence): God gave us eternal life, and this life is in His Son. He who possesses the Son has that life; he who does not possess the Son of God does not have that life. *1 John 5:7-11 (AMP)*

There are three that testify in heaven and on earth as to who Yeshua is. The three in heaven are: Father, the Word and the Holy Spirit. This is the eternal recording of salvation. The Father is love, as the active substance of His unconditional will towards all things. God's love does not change, nor can anything change it. Love is one of the most difficult things for people to experience with a selfish nature. But it is important that self be removed in order for God's perfecting love to cast out all things. Pure love from God shuts that first gateway of the soul which is fear. Man became "afraid" when they heard God's voice. Why fear? Fear is the power of death. As long as fear is present in your life, experiencing the reality of God's love is difficult. Eternal love brings a person into God's presence. Love is the power in the life of a true son. Love is where all worship begins and ends, in and through the Father.

The second witness is the Word. God's word is Truth. God is His word and His word is Himself. When truth is in place, then God's will prevails. Truth is the substance intended by the Lord. Truth is not an idea or philosophical theory. These can only exist because of good and evil. Truth, rather, is based on righteousness. Righteousness is justice, which requires truth. In a courtroom, a witness gets on the stand to tell the truth, the whole truth and nothing but the truth. That witness can speak only the substance of what has happened, not what is going to happen. Right now there is the substance of an event inside of you that has already happened and God's truth wants to bear witness to that. He knew you before you were in your mother's womb. Let that testimony speak that it is there.

It is important to let the will of God come forth by His love. By the same Spirit that resurrected Messiah, so will the Lord's life come and rest in your soul. This is why the soul is a steward. When the testimony of Yeshua comes from heaven, it bears witness to who He is on the earth, according to the life you now have and live. Salvation is the restoration of the soul living in obedience to the Father's will.

The final witness of heaven's testimony is Holy Spirit. Holy Spirit is actually the Spirit of God that ministers Holiness. God tells us to be holy, for He is holy. To be holy is to be set apart for the Lord's purpose. Yeshua was set apart to restore creation, beginning with the salvation of man. The final witness that testifies of Yeshua still does so through His sons, serving as the Lord's representatives. Holiness is about being separated unto the Lord. To be born again is to be separated from the world. It is also to have all that is inside you from the world all the way to Adam separated from you. The Lord restores the soul in order to lead it onto paths of righteousness. It is for the sake of how the Lord functions that righteousness prevails in all things. This is eternal and divine life.

When we look at the Presence of the Almighty One, we must confess there is more to us than what we may think or know. The Father, the Word, and the Spirit bear witness to salvation. They are still bearing witness as the eternal bloodline of those that receive Messiah. Salvation's glory goes all the way down to every cell of the body. What was in the beginning is still now, and is eternal. It NEVER goes away. Nearing the end of His mission on earth, Yeshua asked for the restoration of the glory He had before the world was. Yeshua is the Word – what is more glorious than God's word fulfilling eternal life and its purposes? Our current life is filled with self-corruption and desire, even in our Christian walk. I am not speaking of receiving salvation: I am referring to how salvation is not lived out to the Lord's desired fullness.

Glory is revealed authority. In the prayer of Yeshua recorded in John 17:1-5, we see the request for restoration. Glory is the standard by which authority is revealed. Authority exists because of eternal life. Eternal life begins now, in and through the salvation of Yeshua. The Father gives life eternal because it testifies of the Son through the record of the Holy One. This testimony speaks of the salvation that comes by Yeshua being a son. In Yeshua's obedience, the Word is revealed as the expression of the Father's will on the earth. It is by the Spirit of Holiness that resurrected life occurs. Eternal life is a separation just as much as death is a separation. Salvation restores the Lord's standard of glory. Eternal life is the point of reference for believers.

The Father's glory is reflected in those who are called by the Lord's name. As it is in heaven, so it is on the earth. Glory comes from heaven to earth. The Lord desires to restore what has been missing on the earth: His glory! Beginning with Yeshua, the ultimate example of salvation is a person made to be a son of the Most High. Believers are enabled to know the glory of the begotten One, as well as to know glory at the level of the Lord's salvation, not at the level of religious works.

Below is a chart to illustrate what is available to the true sons of God:

YESHUA'S PRAYER	HEAVEN'S TESTIMONY	BELIEVER'S POSITION	EARTHLY TESTIMONY
GLORY	FATHER	REGENERATED SPIRIT	SPIRIT
AUTHORITY	WORD	RENEWED MIND	WATER
ETERNAL LIFE	HOLY SPIRIT	LIVING SACRIFICE	BLOOD

It is imperative to know that eternal life is now. Salvation is NOW! Salvation of the soul and the regeneration of the spirit is always active. True salvation is never far away or in the "sweet by and by". The reconciliation of salvation makes peace between the Father's will and man's rebellion. When receiving Yeshua's life, the spirit of a person is regenerated. That rebirth brings the testimony of the three that testify in heaven, and renews the three that testify on earth. They are together in the life of the person that receives and lives at this level. They are in you according to the measure of your faithfulness.

There is a sixfold formation of man in salvation through Yeshua. (See previous chart.) This formation is the eternal recording: as it is in heaven, so it is on earth in you. It continues in those that are called sons of God. To be a son, there must be the transformation of everything: mind, will, emotions and body. Believers are joined to the image of the begotten Son. Paul says this clearly in Romans 6:5-11:

> For if we have been united with him in a death like his, we will also be united with him in a resurrection like his. We know that our old self was put to death on the execution-stake with him, so that the entire body of our sinful propensities might be destroyed, and we might no longer be enslaved to sin. For someone who has died has been cleared from sin. Now since we died with the Messiah, we trust that we will also live with him. We know that the Messiah has been raised from the dead, never to die again; death has no authority over him. For his death was a unique event that need not be repeated; but his life, he keeps on living for God. In the same way, consider yourselves to

> be dead to sin but alive for God, by your union with the Messiah Yeshua. *(CJB)*

For the sake of review, let us read the living words of Yeshua again.

> Jesus spoke these things; and lifting up His eyes to heaven, He said, "Father, the hour has come; glorify Your Son, that the Son may glorify You, even as You gave Him authority over all flesh, that to all whom You have given Him, He may give eternal life. This is eternal life, that they may know You, the only true God, and Jesus Christ whom You have sent. I glorified You on the earth, having accomplished the work which You have given Me to do. Now, Father, glorify Me together with Yourself, with the glory which I had with You before the world was. *John 17:1-5*

The hour has come and gone for the Son to be glorified. In all of His glory Yeshua has been revealed. The testimony of heaven has spoken in the life, death, and resurrection of Yeshua. This testimony was there in the beginning when Adam became a living being. Adam made the wrong choice causing his death. Yeshua, the life-giving Spirit, redeems and restores life. Salvation in and through Yeshua brings the testimony of His resurrection into the lives of those who not only receive him, but who, indeed, become sons of God on the earth, living by the testimony of heaven. You must ask yourself: Is your life in agreement with what is being testified in heaven? Are there three witnesses on the earth—the Spirit, the water, and the blood—which manifest heaven's agreement in and through your life as a son?

Glory's standard is in the Father, His Word, and His Spirit. Our response is to live as it is in heaven. We must live like that on the earth too. This new earthen vessel is you. Man is pulled from the ground, now the dust of glory, without the corruption of self: he is "like god". The testimony of God is the greater authority: therefore the authority of man (the DNA of our parents) has no place whereby to rule our lives anymore. Yeshua's life overcomes the record of our ancestors. Our natural DNA is a false record to the born-again believer. We overcome it by the blood of the Lamb and by the words of our testimony. This blood is eternal and God bears witness to it.

A Take-away Thought

Yeshua's prayer speaks of a testimony. His life is an example of what it means to give glory to the Father. God's pattern of salvation is revealed in Yeshua's life. If Yeshua is Lord and King, then there is a definite way by which He expresses His lordship and kingship. There must be an unwavering commitment to him in order for the believer to experience the glory, authority and life eternal. This commitment must remain so powerful that you will endure anything to preserve it. Endurance without bonding will not endure. The Father's sovereignty is the cornerstone of endurance. Endurance that involves absolute resolve for the kingdom of God is a testimony to the majesty of the human spirit. In all that we do, we must endure for the sake of our Father's name; for in doing so, glory is revealed. Ask these questions to ensure your own integrity: Is my fortitude honorable? Does it bring out the best in me? When faced with hardships, do I behave as royalty, walking proudly with my head up, confident in the Lord's strength given to me? Or do I shrink back in fear?

Yeshua withstood the cross because endurance is powered by a life of humility. Godly humility is directed by the Father's will. Humility brings discipline and gives love. Humility focuses in the direction of a glorious kingdom. It is the silent partner of endurance. Although humility is silent, it is not a void. It is a dynamic expression of life that includes love and compassion. Humility is active, not passive. It seeks to join itself to an honorable vision of God's sovereignty. Humility should not be confused with weakness. Yeshua's strength was in His ability to surrender. Yeshua was, is and remains the Lord's strength, living throughout the body of believers.

Eternal life acknowledges qualities and strengths that are not our own. Everything we are and everything we have serves a much higher purpose than the satisfaction of self.

Regardless how small a person is or how large they are in society, everyone is great in the eyes of the Lord because we are made in His image and likeness. The greatness of the Creator is still there, hidden within us. You must learn never to live in the toleration of others but always to live in the celebration of the Lord. In toleration, there will always be warfare. In the celebration of the Lord, there is an abundance of life that produces worship; and worship brings with it glory and honor.

> Therefore if there is any encouragement in Christ, if there is any consolation of love, if there is any fellowship of the Spirit, if any affection and compassion, make my joy complete by being of the same mind, maintaining the same love, united in spirit, intent on one purpose. Do nothing from selfishness or empty conceit, but with humility of mind regard one another as more important than yourselves; do not merely look out for your own personal interests, but also for the interests of others. Have this attitude in yourselves, which was also in Christ Jesus, who, although He existed in the form of God, did not regard equality with God a thing to be grasped, but emptied Himself, taking the form of a bond-servant, and being made in the likeness of men. Being found in appearance as a man, He humbled

Himself by becoming obedient to the point of death, even death on a cross. For this reason also, God highly exalted Him, and bestowed on Him the name which is above every name, so that at the name of Jesus every knee will bow, of those who are in heaven and on earth and under the earth, ^{and} that every tongue will confess that Jesus Christ is Lord, to the glory of God the Father. *Philippians 2:1-11*

A cup that is already filled cannot be filled. But a cup that is empty can hold the difference between life and death. Examine the love in your humility. Believers should avoid tearing down someone's character, starting with their own. As humans, we may not agree on many things but as born-again sons of God, we can rise above self to see ourselves in each other. The Creator of all causes everyone to see everything through His glorious eyes. God loves us in just the same way that He loves His son Yeshua. It is superior to believe this. There is but one vision throughout the many generations that have lived across the nations of the earth. The Lord desires to restore sight to the blind of spirit in order to reveal His glorious kingdom.

You're in the place where your thoughts are. Make sure your thoughts are in the place you want to be. *Reb Nachman of Breslov*

Chapter 2

The Soul

> Then the Lord God formed man of dust from the ground, and breathed into his nostrils the breath of life; and man became a living being.
> *Genesis 2:7*

The soul is man's spiritual bridge between the experiences of the body, the physical world around him and his experience of God. Experience comes through knowledge. Knowing in Hebrew is "yada", meaning the ability to acknowledge. It is to become acquainted with clear understanding. The corruption of knowing good and evil came from a direct experience. Knowing good and evil declares man a god. This "like god" position comes through what is familiar.

In Genesis 4, Adam knew his wife Eve and she conceived. Any experience apart from God can only conceive death, because desire corrupts the soul. The verb for "had relations" or "knew" in Genesis 4:1 is "yada". Knowing causes knowledge. Unless a person partakes of something, there is no knowing it. One can explain or describe something, but unless it is actually engaged with, it is only information. Knowledge in Hebrew is "da'at". *Da'at* is associated with memory and awareness. Knowledge is a power that relies upon recognition. When mankind takes from the tree of good and evil, eyes are opened to the knowledge that is there. There lies the experience which, in turn, creates recognition and thus a memory. This action causes knowing. Consider that, if there is no experience, there can be no memory. When there is recognition, there is sensitivity. Sensitivity has potential consequences. When we are sensitive to something, in most cases, we will react in some way. In our reaction, whether good or bad, there are consequences. Regardless of good or evil, all carnal sensitivity comes from the corrupt soul. The consequence of man's disobedience is desire within the soul. Man is able to see only from the eyes that have generated the realization of good and evil.

Let us look at the etymology of the word *soul* recorded in Genesis 2:7. The soul is "nephesh" in Hebrew. It is the body of life. This body relates to behavior and action. The breath is "neshamah". Who breathed the spirit of Adam? God! The Spirit of God exhales while man receives what is exhaled. What is exhaled? Life! The life that is given is living power. There is also a Hebrew word "ruach" meaning wind, breath or spirit. *Ruach* comes from "rach" which means path. *Ruach* is literally the wind that follows a prescribed path. By extension, *ruach,* or spirit, is the wind of man. The spirit of a person is not just a spiritual entity but it is also his or her character. Character is not just personality but is also atmosphere. Man's spirit is the Lord's atmosphere. Believers are to live in the eternal reality of Spirit wind—"the cool of the day". This atmosphere is the breath of God. STOP! *SELAH.* Look at where the born-again experience puts a person—back with the Spirit wind of God!

The soul is to be the Lord's nature impressed within creation: the Father's "footprints". Man is God's authorized mark on the earth. We have something that cannot be overlooked: the formation of man is unique. God breathes and man becomes a flowing, living spirit being. The Hebrew word for man is *adam* and the word for ground is "adamah". They are identical except for the final Hebrew letter "hei" in the word "adamah". The last letter "hei", in ancient Hebrew pictographs, represents a man with his arms raised. It conveys: to look, reveal, behold, as well as breath. It implies to be in awe of something. When we see something great, there is a small breath of awe. That breath is likened to the meaning of the letter *hei*. *Hei* (hey) has a sound of exhalation which requires a little effort. Adam is formed from the ground (adamah). From *adamah,* God breathes the soul into life and this is "cultivated ground". At the beginning of man's formation (Genesis 2:7) God's life is exhaled and man's nature is made alive. On the cross of the Messiah, mankind is restored by what God exhales of His revealed nature and will in Yeshua. Yeshua breathes His last "exhaling" on the cross while speaking the words: "into Your hands I commit my spirit." He breathes this same "exhaled" breath soon thereafter into the disciples, committing His Spirit into them, and speaking the words: "receive the breath/wind."

> So when it was evening on that day, the first day of the week, and when the doors were shut where the disciples were, for fear of the Jews, Yeshua came and stood in their midst and said to them, "Peace be with you." And when He had said this, He showed them both His hands and His side. The disciples then rejoiced when they saw the Lord. So Yeshua said to them again, "Peace be with you; as the Father has sent Me, I also send you." And when He had said this, He breathed on them and said to them, "Receive the Holy Spirit.
> *John 20:19-22*

Yeshua breathes a breath on the disciples just as His Father had in the formation of man. Yeshua says: "receive the Holy Spirit." This is the true moment of restored life. It is a breath that has destroyed the power of death and releases the power of life.

Having a living soul makes a person a spirit being. Sin-nature breaks away the soul from the Spirit of God. When the soul is fragmented, it cannot carry anything that is eternal. Adam was given the command to tend the garden. This command was the responsibility of guarding the Word of God. Fulfilling the Father's will is guarding His Word. His Word is the ground by which all things are cultivated. A fragmented soul is uncultivated ground. Uncultivated ground has no revelation of life due to its inability to carry life. In Genesis 3:8: "They heard the sound of the Lord God walking in the garden in the cool of the day, and the man and his wife hid themselves from the presence of the Lord God among the trees of the garden." *Cool of the day* is actually the Spirit or "ruach", *that which breathes*. Up until this moment, Adam walked in the Spirit wind. The Lord walked in the breath (the body of life) and the soul of Adam.

The soul is intellectual in nature and contains emotions. At its essence, the soul is knowledge. Knowledge is comprehension. It is what inspires a person to accept or reject a thing, based on understanding. All of man's intelligence knows good and evil. In the soul, the intellect directs thinking. This intellect provides understanding of what is good, what is desired and how to acquire that which is desired. The intellect understands physical-natural concepts; therefore it focuses on the natural. The natural mind includes a religious mind. A religious mind does not mean being spiritually minded. The power of self is knowledge-based and does not reflect what is spiritual. A soul that remains fragmented will always see through the trauma that caused the fragmentation, keeping the person in the natural. The soul will seek to self-legitimize its behavior with reasoning intended to validate its sense of right.

Emotions are, in a sense, one-sided reactions based on what the soul desires. Desire is an appetite that gives strength to what is familiar and will focus on the needs of the "self". Emotions govern action and are based on experience. When the soul is not healed from past hurts, it reacts in the same manner as when the hurt first occurred. Here it is only the familiar operating in order to deceive and separate.

Adam, while making a choice in the garden, was divided within himself. Choice is always a point of division. Choice is to see more than one thing. Choice indicates "self-presence". Self-presence produces self-preservation. Man's free will depends on the intellectual soul. Will includes all modes of behavior: thought, speech and action. These are to be united with God in salvation. Choosing life is not automatic without salvation. Life is to "see God". To see God requires restoration of the soul and to be joined to the image of God's son. The soul, through the Lord's revealing of Himself, is the body of one's spiritual condition. Having been created "in the image of God," man, in his own body and soul, is supremely made to understand the Divinity, upon Whom his very existence is fashioned.

The soul, at its root, is an extension of God's infinite and transcendent being. As an expression of God, the soul attests to the existence of God by virtue of its very being. While clothed by a physical body, the soul continues to assert its eternal origin through its earthly self as well as with the world. Man achieves his expression through will, thought and emotion. Character attributes serve as garments that many people use to dress their souls. If they are unredeemed, or if carnality remains, the soul will remain bound to what is familiar through memory.

The goal of redemption is the complete removal of the old DNA structures, with their tendency towards iniquity and sin, which transgresses God's order. A soul that has not undergone the full process of God's redemption and restoration is still short of heaven's glory. This soul will only engage pleasure and his own will outside the Lord's salvation. Now the soul's power is the intellect and the emotions, which govern conduct and character. Intellect and emotions without a renewed mind have no capacity for divine awareness. In simple vernacular, Adam's choice caused a loss of consciousness: he and Eve "fainted", so to speak. They fell. Man lost the awareness of God, an awareness that man originally had when he was created. Mankind is thus bound to the domains of the soul. Domains are spheres that have been formed by certain influences.

These domains are:
1. Conscience
2. Will
3. Choice

4. Emotion
5. Reasons
6. Imagination

Conscience

Conscience is where the sense of right and wrong exists. It is our integrity, honesty or morality. In our conscience, we establish principles and values. What you value will be your sense of right. This, then, becomes a point of corruption for the soul.

Will

The will is the power of "self-control". Self-control will always be opposed to God's will. Will power is determined by a person's desire. A person's will are his motives and agendas to fulfill his desires. When people are determined to have their way, it is because of the corruption of the soul coming through their will and not the Lord's intended will.

Choice

Choice is the power of decision, based on personal motives and agendas. Personal choice was never part of the Lord's plan for man. Man, in the beginning, operated in the reality of the Lord's will. There was no need to have to make a decision. Before man's action of taking from the tree of knowing good and evil, everything he did was ordered by the Lord's will. Even when the woman acted in eating from the forbidden tree, God's will was still operating in the command He had given to man. We now operate in choice because the soul has experienced the knowledge of good and evil.

Emotion

Emotion is the power of feeling. It is the sensitivity or concern centered on self. A person is never emotional for someone else. Emotionalism may be caused because of someone else, but we can never actually feel what another person is feeling. Emotion is the outer and inner expressions of sentiment towards someone or something. Expressed passion without God is man's "way of right". *Way of right* is the thought of having the "right" to be "like god" in a given situation. When people become emotional, it is because they have determined what they think is good or evil. Corruption of the soul is revealed by a person's emotions. Before sin, emotion did not have a place in the flesh. Emotions should be considered a privilege, not a right.

Reason

Reason is the power of human validity and legitimacy. If something does not make sense, then it cannot be true. And what cannot be true will not fit the paradigm that the soul has made. When we reason through personal understanding we are subjective in viewing life. Human reasoning is "false authority". Without thinking, reason is a veil of deception. Reason becomes the platform for deception. Reason justifies a position by rationalization. Corruption of the soul begins with reason, just as it did in the garden with man.

Imagination

Imagination is the power of vanity through the ego. The ego is the "kingship" of a person. It is through imagination that vanity will form the ego. Imagination is the resourcefulness of the mind. If the mind is not renewed, then imagination will give a false picture. Vanity is self-importance produced from the imagination of a person. Imagination and reason are great playmates. Together they create a sense of good and right. What makes this dangerous is that they are "spiritual"—invisible elements making up the soul. Carnal believers operate in this "soulish" place through the familiar. Vain imaginations darken the heart of a person.

The domains of a soul, without the Lord's sanctification will lead to false light. False light causes false discerning of the spirit.

The soul will discern in the following ways:
1. Pleasure: by gratification
2. Will: by what motivates

3. Intellect: by understanding
4. Character: through personality traits
5. Through the garments of thought and speech

Believers are to worship God with spirit and with truth, since God is Spirit. All obedience is spiritual, whether it is from the soul or from a regenerated spirit through salvation. It is necessary that a born-again person know the truth of the spirit they are operating in. As a born-again person, you must know where you are spiritually according to the Lord's Spirit. The deception of the enemy causes a person to think that their spirit man is engaging the Lord, when, in fact, they are in the realm of the soul. Engaging the Lord requires that you recognize by which domains of the soul you may be operating. All areas within the soul must be restored in order to avoid any false glory. Spiritually, you must know which realm you are occupying. Every part of the soul must go through a redemptive process in order to remove all that may be the familiar.

The soul must be restored to what is known in the Lord. When a person is looking for love in all the wrong places, they will give themselves over mentally and emotionally to their will. Giving at this level is a type of "going out of oneself". When what is given is not valued, then the soul is broken, and that part of you (or that part of your soul) remains in the person or situation that is rejecting you. It is in these areas of brokenness that the familiar attaches itself and trouble develops. It is in brokenness that the soul opens its gateways to the familiar.

Gates of the Soul

There are two main gateways that must be closed in a person's soul. I have mentioned one already. The first opening is fear. Fear has become a part of man's makeup. When man tasted the knowledge of good and evil, there was an immediate shift. This fundamentally defining influence produced a kind of seeing and hearing at the level of "I". "I heard" and became afraid. In Genesis 3:10, we see how fear is man's first gateway opening.

The second gateway we see in Genesis 4:5-7 with the anger of Cain. "But for Cain and for his offering He had no regard. So Cain became very angry and his countenance fell. Then the Lord said to Cain, "Why are you angry? And why has your countenance fallen? If you do well, will not your countenance be lifted up? And if you do not do well, sin is crouching at the door; and its desire is for you, but you must master it." Anger was Cain's wrath giving place to sin. Sin-nature entered through the gateway of Cain's anger. Cain made the choice to not change his face; that is his "perception". As punishment for Cain's action, he is sentenced to wandering.

In Hebrew biblical culture face is an idiom for countenance. Countenance is the visage (face) of man and is mentioned in Genesis 3:19: "By the sweat of your face you will eat bread, till you return to the ground, Because from it you were taken; For you are dust, And to dust you shall return."

The sweat of the brow is the countenance of being "like god" or the toiling that produces it. The seat of intelligence and insight is now man's countenance.

The soul as a being of life was originally able to reveal the Creator through its image and likeness to Him. This was intended to express the dominion of man over creation. Man's soul carried the light of God by which seeing was made possible. At the fall of man, choice brought darkness and the soul began to see through a kingdom of darkness. Cain acted within himself while making the choice to kill his brother. Sin crouched at the door (i.e., opening the gateway to anger) and came in. With blood guilt upon his conscience and the "bloods" of Abel crying out against him from the ground (i.e., the same material as man's formation) Cain's soul and his countenance was narrowed to thought, feeling and will. I say "bloods" because it was not just Abel that was killed but, in fact, all those within Abel also died. Abel's death is the first multi-homicide crime scene in history. Cain was the first serial killer, taking all his victims in one blow. Consider this question: what evil structures were established in that moment? What became of Cain's character as he wandered?

Considering the very first act of aggression ever, after all agendas, motives, causes and explanations used by the ego are removed, all that is left is fear or anger. Fear of the soul is the gate to punishment. Anger of the soul is the gate to wandering. Together they are both acts of separation. Look over your life and remove all the "fluff" and "stuff". What is left will be fear and anger. All conduct that exists is due to these two deeply rooted initial responses. When God's love matures in the soul, fear is cast out. When this love rules and abides, there is acceptance of the Father's will and anger has no place. When fear and anger are left to have their way, all actions give place and power to the enemy and his plan.

Every time a person lives according to the flesh—pride, lust, anger, jealousy, envy, lies, laziness, perversion, procrastination, worry, acts of disobedience, vanity, imaginations—it is by choice. Choice is the voice of deception within an unredeemed person. When we choose to satisfy the flesh, Satan is consuming us through carnal desire, which gives him place in the soul and activity of the body. The place given to Satan gets recorded in time and becomes part of the DNA history of a family's bloodline. Through desire and the falling into his temptation, the enemy and his kingdom increase in power and territory on the earth. This is why flesh and blood cannot inherit the kingdom of God. Yeshua said to eat of his body and to drink of his blood. In communion with the Lord, in faithfulness to His word, and with the unwavering trust of the heart, there is a change in the soul and body. The Word of God is made alive and actively seeks to expose and destroy every hidden work of the enemy, indeed all the way back to eternity.

The physical makeup of the body engages the senses of taste, sight, hearing, touch and smell. All acts that come through flesh become a sin-covering from which Satan is able to rule. Satan hides in the desires of a person through "self". The object for which you forsake the Lord is the price at which Satan buys your soul. Whatever is in your soul that causes you to abandon the Lord's will is the point where the enemy gives his gratification. Whatever is gained from abiding in the realm of choice, Satan, as the prince of this world, exchanges the pleasure in the choice. But there is a price that comes with this exchange.

> For the wages of sin is death, but the free gift of God is eternal life in Christ Jesus our Lord.
> *Romans 6:23*

There are wages paid in exchange for gaining the world, though there is no profit. To sin is to work for death. To live is to be given eternal life in the lordship of Yeshua. Eternal life is a gift. There is nothing that can be done to earn eternal life. Freedom is serving in the Lord's kingdom. It is sad to think that people are working themselves to death for the temporal.

The intellect, consciousness, subconscious, emotions, and desires are all forms of reasoning that comprise the false covering of self. DNA is the book of life that carries all that has happened in a person's life throughout time. When you stand before the Lord, it is not just you He sees. The Lord can look down into the whole history of a person. As Creator of everything, He knows every generation that has ever lived before a person. Every generation is also still standing before Him. Without salvation, sin-nature (even generational) remains in the desire of the soul. The soul is where human desire resides. Paul says in Romans 7:18-25:

> For I know that nothing good dwells within me, that is, in my flesh. I can will what is right, but I cannot perform it. [I have the intention and urge to do what is right, but no power to carry it out.] For I fail to practice the good deeds I desire to do, but the evil deeds that I do not desire to do are what I am [ever] doing. Now if I do what I do not desire to do, it is no longer I doing it [it is not myself that acts], but the sin [principle] which dwells within me [fixed and operating in my soul]. So I find it to be a law (rule of action of my being) that when I want to do what is right *and* good, evil is ever present with me *and* I am subject to its insistent demands. For I endorse *and* delight in the Law of God in my inmost self [with my new nature]. But I discern in my bodily members [in the sensitive appetites and wills of the flesh] a different law (rule of action) at war against the law of my mind (my reason) and making me a prisoner to the law of sin that dwells in my bodily organs [in the sensitive

appetites and wills of the flesh]. O unhappy *and* pitiable *and* wretched man that I am! Who will release *and* deliver me from [the shackles of] this body of death? O thank God! [He will!] through Jesus Christ (the Anointed One) our Lord! So then indeed I, of myself with the mind *and* heart, serve the Law of God, but with the flesh the law of sin. *AMP*

The human soul has a threefold cord that is not easily broken:
1. Lust of the flesh
2. Lust of the eye
3. Pride of life

"To be like God" is what the serpent promised for knowing good and evil. Being like God can only come through human desire. This desire is what infected man's eternal nature. The enemy's cord represents where his power resides: in the realm of desire and not in the will of God. Desire exists in order to make the flesh known. Flesh is a covering that darkens the soul. Desire that is confined to the knowledge of good and evil is under the control of Satan. The power of the enemy resides in a person's conformity to what they want. Without desire, sin has no place to dwell. Without desire, sin has no power to tempt: there is no temptation in salvation because God cannot be tempted. Temptation is an appeal to something that is not present. Temptation is the enticement for self-gratification—which, more than likely, is an immediate gratification. When all we are belongs to the Father, then human desire no longer exists. All that remains is the Father's will.

> And you were dead in your trespasses and sins, in which you formerly walked according to the course of this world, according to the prince of the power of the air, of the spirit that is now working in the sons of disobedience. Among them we too all formerly lived in the lusts of our flesh, indulging the desires of the flesh and of the mind, and were by nature children of wrath, even as the rest. But God, being rich in mercy, because of His great love with which He loved us, even when we were dead in our transgressions, made us alive together with Christ (by grace you have been saved), and raised us up with Him, and seated us with Him in the heavenly places in Christ Jesus, so that in the ages to come He might show the surpassing riches of His grace in kindness toward us in Christ Jesus. For by grace you have been saved through faith; and that not of yourselves, it is the gift of God; not as a result of works, so that no one may boast. For we are His workmanship, created in Christ Jesus for good works,

which God prepared beforehand so that we would walk in them. *Ephesians 2:1-10*

Ego

Ego is self-image, self-worth and even self-esteem. Ego keeps the soul in bondage through pride and denial. There is a cycle within the soul that will build the personality. Through this personality, the body forms the ego or the life out of which people live. It is a place designed by what is familiar. The cycles of the familiar are recorded and give strength to the ego. All dysfunctions, malfunctions and break-downs in the soul (mind, will and emotions) affect the body. As for fear and anger, these two legitimize what is credible and defend what is justifiable within the ego. Ego cares about the way things appear on the outside. And because of this caring, all perception comes through the veil of ego.

The demonic formula that creates the demonic structure is: fear + anger = ego. Fear says, "I must control this or..." Anger says, "I have the right so..." The power of deception is based on fear and anger. Ask yourself: how many times have you hidden your true heart because of fear? Now ask yourself: how many times have you denied your true heart because of anger? Deeply hidden under all that is Satan's plan to provoke human desire—all in order to bring forth his hidden objective, to satisfy the "I". Desire is the veil of darkness within the soul. Ego is the outward expression of inner desire. The eyes that were opened in the garden became the garment of darkness that has covered man's true being. Under the hidden realm of desire there is still the Lord's revelation that stands as the original covering. It should be noted that man's first self-guided act was to *cover*.

All human effort—any labor of human power, pride or self-will used to gain spiritual liberty—is the religious activity of "I". Natural knowledge desires to manipulate. Manipulation is influence in a particular direction. Most likely, it is a self-centered persuasion with hidden motives and agendas. When pride or self-will is operating, is really has influence over a person. Manipulation is man's way of pulling towards what, in fact, is controlling him. Such a way of living is subject to narrow human viewpoints and will be faulty. In dominion over creation, the soul exists as the right to life versus the right to choose. Disobedience transformed man from a simple being to a being that has to make choices, which makes disobedience an option. The awareness of being naked shaped perception because of the deceptive nature of sin. The power of sin within the soul is desire. Desire blinds and binds man to flesh. Flesh-nature delights in the fruit of sin. The fruit of sin bends the will of man into serving. Sin then becomes the influence or master of the soul. This is the "old man" or the sum total of what was inherited from Adam.

When the Lord looks at a person, He sees the lifetime within that person standing before Him. When the enemy seeks to accuse the person, his mind bears witness (evidence) to the place in which he gained access. When trying to bring an indictment, there must be evidence found against the person. For Satan, the strongest evidence in a generation is its bloodline. Simply put: "Is there DNA at the scene of the crime?" The DNA is the book of life that serves as the blueprint of a person. Adam is in every person and every person is in Adam. The living soul man was created to be in the image and likeness of God. Without the Lord's redemption, he carries the guilty verdict because Adam committed the crime of choice by desire. This choice changed our capacity to reveal glory. It altered seeing and transformed the core of our spiritual being.

All that has taken place since the introduction of choice is the practice of sin-nature. The human soul, which is by nature without redemption, actively shifts based on desire. By removing the power of desire, the soul is restored to the revealed glory of God. The soul is once again a being of life and no longer a being of lies. What you desire spiritually will be reflected through the soul. Just as you are what you eat physically, so your soul is what it is by receiving the bread of life through the Spirit. Man's senses are means of perception in order to gain perspective. Sight, hearing, taste, smell and touch form the image which a soul will live out. It is critical that believers guard the image of the Lord.

God is Spirit and it is taught that He has no physical image. This is true but it is not fully accurate. Yeshua is the expressed image of an invisible God, according to Colossians

1:15. There is a visible image of God and it is the entire lifetime of a believer. Though not physical, God's glory is revealed in how salvation is lived out in the lives of those called by His nature. Notice that I said "nature" and not *name*. In Hebrew tradition, names carry a function and express intention, nature and character. Yeshua gives an example of this to the disciples when teaching them how to pray in Matthew 6:9-10. He says: "Our Father in heaven! May your Name be kept holy. May your Kingdom come, your will be done on earth, as in heaven." (CJB) In practice, what Yeshua is saying is: "May God's name be holy by the way life is lived." Then immediately God's kingdom comes and the earth is filled with the Lord's glory. The soul must undergo the Lord's glorious refining process in order to experience freedom and faithfulness. The Lord's glory is His righteousness that brings truth and justice. Righteousness is the seed of all fullness. Peace restores the soul of a person, as a true son reflecting the Father's glory.

Fear and anger are gates to the soul. The poor in spirit are fearful or angry people. More often than not, the poor in spirit live in the broken places of their soul. It is through ego that fear and anger wreak havoc upon a person's perception. The two doors that must be closed are fear and anger. Love removes all fear and destroys the work of anger.

Desire: The Deepest Deception

> When the woman saw that the tree was good for food, and that it was a delight to the eyes, and that the tree was desirable to make one wise, she took from its fruit and ate; and she gave also to her husband with her, and he ate. Then the eyes of both of them were opened, and they knew that they were naked; and they sewed fig leaves together and made themselves loin coverings. *Genesis 3:6-7*

Desire is a "first person" principle. Adam is the first blood person; the first embodiment of eternal life; the first one able to reflect the Creator of life. As the first person, Adam has no awareness of self; therefore he has no awareness of his own nakedness. Self is a revealed state. Self is the result of knowing good and evil, starting with the first man, Adam (male and female). By such layers, man (male/female) sees less. Desire is fed by knowing good and evil. Partaking of the tree in the beginning imparted the reality of good and evil as opposed to the truth.

Human desire engages what is false, which is based on self-centered wants. Desire removes our eternal value and brings with it religious values, moral values, political values and intellectual values. All these values give place to good and evil. In giving up his place, man loses glory, authority and eternal life. As a result of this loss, desire creates a pleasure/value conflict. People, in general, value what they desire. In the beginning there was no desire, but only love. Love is the substance that reveals what is eternal. Love is what caused the initial separation from God. When the male took from his wife the "forbidden" fruit, it was out of love. Love was the only thing in existence. There was no hate at this point. When the male took from his wife, it was from himself. Male and female were identical, made in God's in image and likeness. There was no male image or female likeness. God created "them" male and female, in His image and likeness. It is important to remember that male and female are one as a spirit-being, but function according to their divinely given design. As spirit-beings, there is no difference as far as substance is concerned. There is no distinction as we know it. Man's love for his wife caused his actions. God's love for His creation restores the ability to know eternal life, or the life that is recorded within every person made as an image and likeness of God. Man is to perceive, and reflect on, once again the original Genesis 1:26-28 mandate.

Looking back at the beginning, it is the desire that gives place to deception. Desire changed man's nature. Desire is to take pleasure in something.

The Lord perceives everything but not everything is a part of him. Satan's desire was to be above God. His desire was his deception. This is why desire has the function of deception. Desire is rebellious because it rejects God's will. Satan did not know his rebellion would change his place until it happened. And if it happened once, it can happen again. The enemy and his rebellious substance form the authority by which he is allowed to rule.

Satan, as a created being, lost his original purpose. His desire was, and remains, intentional. The enemy comes to steal, kill and destroy (John 10:10). The god of this world blinds the mind of man so that the light of the gospel is hidden. Desire brings with it insurrection, which causes all things to be changed from the Lord's original intent and purpose. Salvation brings resurrection, which recovers what was lost. The knowledge of good and evil is only in the perception of Adam, but not within his original make-up. Adam partakes of the tree of knowing good and evil, but this was not the Lord's original plan for man. Adam took something that was outside and brought it inside himself. Knowing good and evil became a part of man.

When looking at desire, we must look at the nature of the mind and our mental attitudes. These attitudes shape personality. Personality is both person and personal. The enemy was able to successfully change how Adam saw everything. This awareness then created his self-image through the experience of knowing good and evil. Good and evil began to be cultivated when thinking about what was right and what was wrong. It is in self-determining right and wrong that the underlining structures of our personality are formed. These structures include beliefs, values, ideas, as well as past and present culture, all of which continuously permit cyclical patterns of life, both constructive and destructive. Desire is not God's will if it is still confined to just knowing good and evil.

Desire is a power. Whatever you value will be the substance of what will come into being, and therefore affects your being. Whatever affects you is power. Power is the influence created. Influence is control. Control is authority. When we partake of something that we know is not the Father's will, we give power to it by our desire for it. Desire is the power of our sin-nature. Without desire sin-nature has no power. Sin is a nature but the power of that nature is the corruption of human desire. The nature of a person stems from what is desired, as it is defined by good and evil.

Desire is grounded in the will of a person. This will is considered by some to be "free will". Exercising will brings a sense of freedom, but there is no true freedom apart from God. Self-will is a function of desire and it puts volition into the hands of what or who controls it. It is not sin that attracts a person; it is desire that distracts from the Lord's will. The nature of desire is to attract, appeal or entice. Desire is parallel to motivation. Because desire is the enemy's tool, he must corrupt the heart of a person. It is in the heart that emotions and plans for actions exist. Desire causes people to become emotional and act out. An unredeemed person has an unidentified history in his bloodline that causes emotions and actions. These "emotional" accounts create personalities. These personalities are the character traits that can resist

God's purposes and plans as well as His love, and often also His will. People can be deceived by their own intentions. Have you ever watched children do something that imitates their parents? Well, where did that behavior come from? How can a child display a mannerism of a parent unless there is a record stored somewhere in the child? While it is true that environment does shape behavior, personality is genetic. Genes are the inheritable factor within a person. Genes tell all, including the actions of a person's past. All the choices and actions are recorded in a person. If these choices or actions are not in accordance with the Lord's will then the consequences will be passed on to a child through genetic material. This may seem impossible but in actuality man is the first and ultimate memory chip.

Intention and *belief* are not synonymous. *Belief* is an acceptance based on a trusted conviction. It is certainty with or without the experience of a truth. *Intention* is a function of an aim or purpose. In a mind that is not renewed by a relationship with God, belief and intention fall short of life in the eternal. Together, belief and intention will work in conjunction with the familial and the familiar. Left unresolved, desire gives pride a place in which to hide. Anything that can hide will never operate according to the Lord's will. Whatever is for the Lord will always be pure and without shame. Whatever is pure will always reflect the Father's will through His nature.

Desire corrupts the soul and helps motivate intention. Motivation and intention are the substance of pride. Emotion is being feeling-based. Emotions are always directed toward something or someone. There is never a time when emotions have no place. Emotions are either within a person or directed outside, towards something or someone else. Because emotions are strongly connected to desire, a person will make unsound decisions which cut them off from the Lord's spiritual identity and eternal destiny. Any behavior that is based on desire comes from knowing good and evil.

All religious actions motivated by personal desire are not God-centered, even though they are disguised as good intentions. Let me reiterate: when I say "religious" I am referring to the religion of "I". All that is in the world today is the "I" or the "like God" religion of self. This is how man becomes "like God", determining what is good and what is evil based on desire. This principle can be applied to every area of life: socially, politically, educationally and economically. Look at the world around us: every perceivable thing is because of what is either good or evil. This interpretation will differ based on personality and intention. You must look directly at your heart and confront all corruption caused by human desire. You must also examine what you believe in and determine where it comes from. Is the salvation you so strongly confesses free of all personal desire? Is salvation daily manifesting in you because of the Lord's presence? Desire, coupled with wrong beliefs, will weaken your walk with the Lord.

Carnal desire will always be directed towards what is valued; it is the same with belief. This is what happened with the woman and the serpent. The woman believed something which caused her to have desire. Belief transcends all dimensions of time: past, present and future. Belief never needs desire but rather desire will always need something to believe in. A person can always believe that something *is* the case, but what a person desires is that something *be* the case. If the soul is not purified from the carnal desire, a person can hinder the true work of the Lord's salvation in his life.

A lifetime is a life that is lived out in the reality of time. When we look at unredeemed life, we must see it as part of time. Time is a period of connected moments, seasons, occasions and phases. Time is filled with events that occur in irreversible succession, from the past through the present, and towards the future. Why is it so important that we know this? It is because desire and time work together. Desire is subject to time. Time can make desires strong or weak. Time can make a person "dependent" on being independent. Dependence is connected to control. Whatever it is you depend on will control you. You become passive and responsible to that which is controlling you. Being independent is to operate from the awareness of self, depending on whatever it is you desire. Living life as a responsible person is a *world system* concept. In the beginning we were not responsible for creation; that was God's responsibility as the Creator of it all. In the beginning we were responsive to creation through the command from God to "tend" it.

Creation is still waiting for this to happen in order to fulfill its part, so that all will be filled with God's glory.

Human will, by nature, opposes God's will. Living by the will of the Father, as it is revealed through Yeshua, requires that we give up all claims to the function of personal desire, which, in turn, gives up all that desire claims within the soul. The will is the action of a person's set disposition. Being a son requires that there be nothing that can claim our God life. *God life* is life that reveals the record of God's glory. It is the honor of the righteous and the revelation of God's kingdom. God life requires absolute conviction. It means looking at the soul and seeing as the Lord sees.

Conviction is Holy Spirit's point of contact in the broken areas of the soul which brings about a higher awareness of the Lord. Conviction does not mean repentance. Conviction means the person has been made aware that there is an area that has transgressed the holiness of God. The first confession of Yeshua is a confession of recognizing where we are—that is, separated from the Lord. This is a sinner's admission. We are then admitted into the Father's kingdom through His son. Though we enter into the Lord's kingdom for "free", a price has been paid. When a person acknowledges where they are—that is, apart from God—then the confession of sin can begin. We confess sin as it is revealed in the light of the Lord's holiness.

The conviction of the Holy Spirit can be compared to a bruise. Often we have bruises on our body without noticing their initial cause. It is not until we press on the bruise that we feel sore. It is then that we realize that there is a bruise. We may stop and wonder when we received it but we rarely remember. Therefore we don't take the bruise seriously. Likewise, the Holy Spirit acts as that gentle "bump" against the soul that makes us aware there is an injury in us somewhere, and that we need to look at it. With each look, we are made aware of what is in need of healing. It is more than a "one-time" altar confession. It is a *process* of being made whole so that the Lord's glory can be fully reflected in every area of our being.

I want to use my own life as an example of being whole. As a child I did not have the best experience. There was physical abuse, which caused my soul (mind, will and emotions) to be broken. In time, as I grew up, I lived out of that place of being abused. I made decisions, acted and thought from that place. Until I truly received the Lord's salvation, all I did stemmed from a religious self. I even thought that going to church would somehow cover up my true heart of pain, shame and guilt. I had determined what was a "good" thing to do, and in doing so, I lived out of a false relationship with the Lord and with other people. I have always thought religion is something people believe in order to make them feel like they are "right" with God. But this is self-determined. My proof of this was how I felt towards my family. I did not reflect the Father's forgiveness or kindness whatsoever. There was my evidence. The "I" in me created a principle for myself that determined what was good and what was evil. Deceived by my carnal desire, I failed in the Lord's salvation because I had made salvation fit into my life. My soul was still shattered and the memory of my abused childhood prevailed. Like a broken mirror, I lived through the shards of the past instead of through the wholeness of my eternal destiny and spiritual identity in the Lord.

I am not saying to live your life always looking for what is wrong with you. I am stating that salvation is an ongoing, restorative relationship with the Lord. This relationship must touch every part of your being: past, present and future. According to the nature of salvation, believers have the right to call their soul back from all the places where it has been broken. An unredeemed soul will live in the memory of what caused the brokenness. The nature of self-preservation, then, produces dysfunctions that fragment the soul. These dysfunctions remain, unless the soul is restored to God's love. Have you ever experienced a bad marriage that ended in an ugly divorce? Are the memories of the relationship good, evil or forgiven?

Let's stop here and do a simple exercise that can begin the process of restoring the soul. Close your eyes and take time to allow the Holy Spirit to speak to your areas of pain and loss. Look to see if there are any memories that unsettle you. Are there people that have deeply hurt you? Do you still get a "sting" thinking about them? Do you still have memories that cause you to behave in a certain way? If you see a person in your mind, what is your heart towards them? If any of these questions are not answered in the light and love of God, then your soul is fragmented. This is not about salvation. I am speaking of restoring your saved soul. As long as there are unresolved issues, the enemy has a place in you and is able to keep you separated from God's fullness for you right now. Believers are now seated in the Messiah. Your life is hidden NOW! Now is salvation! It is not in the by-and-by that the kingdom comes. God's kingdom is here NOW, in Yeshua. Your spirit is regenerated and your soul is restored to the capacity of eternal glory. You must live to engage and administrate at this level.

I encourage you to daily call your soul back into alignment with the Father's perfect will. After calling your soul back into alignment, you will see the Lord renew your mind. When your mind is renewed, it sees according to the Father who is revealing Himself within you. The Lord reveals Himself at the particular place and time where a soul has been restored. Then your decisions are no longer human choices but are the Father's will since they are a supernatural response to Him. There are no struggles of the flesh because the soul is functioning in redemption. If being saved is indeed redemption, then why is the soul not automatically renewed? People still have the same old habits (due to old thought patterns, will and emotions) because their soul is not yet fully restored to the level of God's purposed glory for them.

The enemy was able to condemn me because I carried the guilt of unforgiveness towards my family. But thanks be to God, today I see clearly and recognize all too well the damage condemnation can bring if left to its own devices. Memory will create an image. A soul that is left with a bad memory will create a bad image. Blame will condemn a person and leaves no room for forgiveness because blame itself stands guilty. There is a difference between conviction and condemnation. Conviction brings repentance—meaning that it causes a turning towards the Lord. This turning is the "repentance" that brings us into the Lord's truth and righteous living. Condemnation, on the other hand, does the exact opposite. Condemnation brings a further separation from the Lord. It is easy to know the difference between conviction and condemnation. Always ask yourself this question: "Does my new awareness lead me towards God's love and forgiveness, causing me to change and to be restored? Or does the new awareness lead me further into shame, guilt, fear, excuses and justification?" The source of a thing will determine its potential. And this potential will become the actuality of the source.

Take-away Thought

Most people spend a lifetime struggling in their soul. A person must deal with the corruption of human desire to be freed from darkness. These struggles come from needing answers or solutions to the issues of a fragmented soul. Peace can never come at a person's demand when it comes to the

Lord. The person must surrender all for the Lord to make everything complete. Surrender means to no longer have an opinion about anything. Surrender is that silence within the soul that is able to wait on the Lord. It takes time and patience to get to this place, especially after generations of conversations have taken place with the enemy within the heart.

When it comes to the Lord's will, we must seek Him with His heart in mind. If we seek Him, He will be found, but it must be His way and not our way. Most people ask only for what they feel they have the right to ask for. Most people want the Lord to relieve them of the symptom of a pain or problem when it is really the cause that must be addressed. A *kingdom question* must be asked in order to get a *kingdom answer*. A kingdom question is: "Who am I in the realm of Your Spirit?" Or "Who was I before I received sin-covering?" There is a timeless record that carries an answer. Salvation is the testimony that has conquered all things in time, and should not be thought of as something to come in the future.

Salvation is deeper than the soul because it involves the regeneration of the spirit. In regeneration, there is the awakening of our spirit to the Father. The soul is the access point not for the body but for the spirit man to connect to the earth through redemption. Satan torments us at the level of an unredeemed soul. Demon in Greek is "daimonion". It is an evil spirit. It comes from the word "daimon", from *daio*. *Daio* means "to distribute destinies". This means that Satan wants to change the eternal destiny of mankind. The kingdom of darkness seeks to establish itself in order to gain power. It is through illegal "search-and-seizure" that mankind loses all that the Lord gave. At the end of everything, the Lord is still asking "Where are you?" The question is "where" because there is a place of separation in which the unredeemed die. Satan wants people's destiny because destiny is determined through what a person desires and their choices. If the enemy has what a person desires, then he influences their choice – this is power for him.

Since the very beginning of desire (in the Garden of Eden), fear and anger have reproduced after their kind through generational bloodlines. With each generation, the soul of that generation becomes more fragmented by the familiar. The kingdom of darkness wants to keep people in the familiar through the words of the liar. So much opportunity for the Lord's glory to have preeminence in creation is lost due to the unrenewed mind. Instead of a generation going from glory to glory, the generation goes from story to story, and Satan is the storymaker.

Redemption of the soul is the re-establishment of the Father's glory in mankind. There is an eternal record with a supernatural wisdom and the Father's love. It is the eternal Father speaking you—into His spiritual lineage. The restoration of man's soul is required for the regeneration of the spirit. Psalm 23:3 says: "He restores my soul; He guides me in the paths of righteousness For His name's sake." A soul is redeemed for the sake of God's character and nature. When a soul is restored properly, it is no longer fragmented. It is able to know God's justice. After salvation, time and the debt of time no longer work against the eternal record that has been dormant in a person. Knowing the truths of life comes through relationship with the Father. Each moment of born-again life should not be a constant struggle with sin issues. But each born-again moment is the continued removal of all the "fig leaves" so that what is underneath is gloriously and righteously revealed, expressing the Father's love and faithfulness. The fig leaf is man's idea of a good first covering. However, this action of covering up fell short of the glory of God.

> Then the eyes of both of them were opened, and they knew that they were naked; and they sewed fig leaves together and made themselves loin coverings. *Genesis 3:7*

Figs leaves are mentioned several times in the New Testament as hints for redemption. In the beginning, fig leaves were used to cover the actions of choice. Fig leaves represent the false covering used in the garden where man attempted to cover his act of disobedience; much like it is with religious works. Fig leaves represent the covering of human DNA, the record of our ancestors. All this false covering is inherited "fruit". In Mark 11 Yeshua speaks to a fig tree full of leaves and declares never again will man eat of this tree, which is symbolic of "knowledge". Knowledge of good and evil produces a form of "self" which, in reality, is an illusion compared to the true representation that man is to reflect as an image and likeness of God.

The fig tree is mentioned again in John 1:48 with Nathanael. Yeshua addresses the false covering when He tells Nathanael *I saw you under the fig tree*. Again, Yeshua is dealing with man's initial act of hiding. Yeshua's obedience removes the "leaves" under which shame and nakedness hide. Salvation restores godly perception by giving life, and man's true sight and insight. The experience of knowing good and evil is no longer part of a born-again person because he is now a new creation. Everything that caused a person to hide in personality (the familiar) or experience (the familial) then ceases to be based in knowing good and evil. All "fig leaf" coverings are destroyed in the work of the cross.

God's presence is beyond good and evil; therefore He cannot be experienced by the standards of knowing good and evil. Knowledge of good is still forbidden knowledge. Knowledge of evil is still forbidden knowledge. "I" is the religion of knowing good and evil and this is still forbidden. All deception comes to steal, kill and destroy the Lord's glory. Man is the crown of God's creation. The crown of man is the will of the Lord. The will of the Lord is always expressed in His love and kindness. Living according to the Father's will honors the Father's glory.

> "To be a person of truth, be swayed neither by approval nor disapproval." *Reb Nachman of Breslov*

Chapter 3

Glory and the Regenerated Spirit

> He said, "Father, the hour has come; glorify Your Son, that the Son may glorify You. ...Now, Father, glorify Me together with Yourself, with the glory which I had with You before the world was. *John 17:1, 5*

What a wonderful prayer! "Glorify me together with Yourself, with the glory that was before the world existed." Experiencing God's glory is, indeed, overwhelming in thought but is in fact a reality in Yeshua. Glory refers to the origin of the soul. Yeshua knew the story of man because He had come in the likeness of men. He sympathized with man's weaknesses, having been tempted in all things yet He was without sin. Yeshua lived His life for the glory of His Father. Throughout His life, He made no reputation of Himself. When seeking to know the glory of salvation, one begins with making no reputation of oneself. It is the absolute surrendering of all self-seeking desire. The ultimate example of this is Yeshua's death on the cross. He became selfless through His obedience.

The soul is the vessel carrying the very nature of God. This cannot be underestimated in salvation for us born-again spirit beings.

> So when it was evening on that day, the first day of the week, and when the doors were shut where the disciples were, for fear of the Jews, Yeshua came and stood in their midst and said to them, "Peace be with you." And when He had said this, He showed them both His hands and His side. The disciples then rejoiced when they saw the Lord. So Yeshua said to them again, "Peace be with you; as the Father has sent Me, I also send you." And when He had said this, He breathed on them and said to them, "Receive the Holy Spirit.
> *John 20:19-22*

I am repeating John 20:19-22 on purpose. Take note of what happens after the resurrection of Yeshua. He says "Peace be with you" and breathes on His disciples. What is going on here? Yeshua says to receive the Holy Spirit. The breath He breathes has overcome the world and has conquered death and the grave. Sin-nature is completely and absolutely destroyed. Iniquity has no power. There is no transgression against God because of obedience.

There is a parallel to the first day of the week when Yeshua speaks *Peace be with you* to His disciples. It connects back to the first day of creation. Genesis 1:5: "...And there was evening and there was morning, one day." In the Hebrew text, the words used for "one day" is "echad yom". It is not just the first sequential day for creation. The first day consists of evening and morning. These are two opposite states that are joined to function as one day. All of creation is unified, according to the days of creation, as expressed in the separation of light and darkness.

The corresponding first day, at the beginning of Genesis, is reflected by the Spirit separating darkness from light. The wind of the Spirit is reconciling. Yeshua is one with God because He is glorified in His resurrection. Yeshua's "salvation" makes all things full and complete as "one" fully revealed Light. Yeshua (salvation) is the revelation of all things. The eyes that understand the "knowledge of good and evil" are closed, so that, through the eyes of the Spirit, "knowing" is once again an awareness of the glory in God. In the entirety of man (spirit, soul and body), nothing is separate from the Lord.

Salvation says, "I am with you always." Always with you is the consolation that "there is nothing that can separate the redeemed from the Lord." This is because of the power that lies in the resurrected life of Yeshua and His glory.

Salvation reconciles and restores. It engages the Spirit by the breath of God. Salvation takes a person into the Lord's presence and then conforms him into the image of His son. True worship opens the inner man to all that is holy within the Lord. Where a heart begins to revere the Lord's presence, there will be glory. Many believers fall short of knowing the truth of the Spirit in which they are to worship. Romans 3:23 says: "for all have sinned and fall short of the glory of God." Where is man's (male and female) first position? Glory! Romans 3 states that "being justified is a gift by His grace through the redemption which is in Christ Yeshua." In the complete Jewish Bible version, it is put this way, starting with verse 22:

> And it is a righteousness that comes from God, through the faithfulness of Yeshua the Messiah, to all who continue trusting. For it makes no difference whether one is a Jew or a Gentile, since all have sinned and come short of earning God's praise. By God's grace, without earning it, all are granted the status of being considered righteous before him, through the act redeeming us from our enslavement to sin that was accomplished by the Messiah Yeshua. *Romans 3:22-24 (CJB)*

The soul is essentially the path where the Lord's Spirit walks, revealing Himself while also separating all darkness that causes man to fall short of what the Lord reveals—His "glory". The power of the soul is to act as the "tongue" or the language of God Himself on the earth. Our soul carries the message of what the Lord intends. Yeshua's breath carries the revelation of His Father. Reconciliation is breathed upon the disciples by the function of salvation as "WORD", which then transforms their souls by the "wind" of God's glory. The resurrection is the exaltation of the Lord. It is not just an event but an actual place. Yeshua's life, in His breath, has the eternal life that exists in the Father's revealed glory. Image and likeness in authority is restored. Life eternal is received and known. Man's soul is no longer captivated by self-desire since the Father's will has found a place again in the hearts of those that receive restoration of their souls. Man regains the awareness and experience of God. The ultimate unity of the soul in God is manifested by pure faith, absolute devotion and the continuous readiness to sacrifice one's life for God, as Yeshua has done as our example.

Repentance and Returning Glory

Regeneration is the catalyst for repentance. When man's spirit is made alive, the immediate response is repentance. Repentance can mean more than one thing, depending on the time and place. There is only one message recorded in the

Bible. There is only one message for mankind. It is a clarion call to repent! Return! From the beginning, the Lord has had but one desire: and that is to have His creation restored to His perfect will. Salvation and the kingdom of heaven are directly linked to this return.

> From that time Jesus began to preach and say, Repent, for the kingdom of heaven is at hand.
> *Matthew 4:17*

Biblical repentance is a misinterpreted concept outside biblical culture. Repentance in today's mainstream thinking means believing in Yeshua or "getting saved". Repentance is a "me and my" salvation experience. By the Greek definition, repentance is the changing of one's mind. By observation, repentance is the real change of mind and attitude toward sin and toward the cause of it (not merely the consequences of it), which affects one's whole life and not merely a single act within it.

To understand repentance in the context of the Bible, an examination of Scripture written before Yeshua' lifetime is required. It is a clear fact that there was no written New Testament when the message of repentance was being preached. In fact, the first messages of repentance did not address the Gentiles, but Israel herself. John the Baptist, Yeshua and eventually Peter all proclaimed the same message. As Jewish men, they brought the first message of repentance to the nation of Israel, within the cultural and political understanding of the day. This does not negate the message of truth of Yeshua for us today, but we need to be aware of the subject of repentance in all the fullness of God's intention for it, as it relates to biblical history as well as its relevancy for believers today.

The first message the kingdom of heaven brings us concerns a covenant and a people called to this covenant. Israel as a nation, as a people of great history, had undergone numerous periods of prosperity and exile. They had a clear understanding of who they were. They had witnessed nations rise and fall as a result of who they were under the God of their forefathers. According to the text of Matthew 4, the Roman Empire was ruling in the land promised to Abraham. Time and history had infiltrated God's treasured possession to the point where His people had turned into a nation alienated within their land. With the outside influences of Persia, Greece and Rome encroaching in power more and more over the few hundred years prior to the arrival of Yeshua, Israel had adapted to economic and social structures of invading nations. Israel had become a nation influenced by pagan cultures. The cry of repentance was not a cry to accept a Messiah so much as a cry to return to their first love; a call to the covenant made on Mt. Sinai; a plea to honor the promise their forefathers had made with the One True Living God.

For the children of Israel, repentance was about a truth and a righteousness that had been revealed in relationship with a covenant-making God and His Torah. John, Yeshua and Peter were men well acquainted with the Torah, or God's instruction. The Torah was about a way of life that was to demonstrate the covenant with the Lord. This law was not for the salvation of Israel. If this were true, then the Lord could have given the Torah and Israel would have been "saved" from Egypt through the Torah. This was not the case. Israel was freed from Egyptian bondage first; and then God's instructions came afterwards. The mistake made by non-Jewish believers was to see the law as a way of salvation. Once Israel was free and had agreed to follow the Lord in His ways, they became a holy nation again by the way they lived. The path to walk was there for them, but it was relationship that was the most important aspect of their covenant. Walking with the Lord is one thing. How people walk when leaning on their own understanding of the Lord is another. This was the case for Israel in the covenant they had with the Lord.

The language of the Gospels is not about believing in Yeshua but rather about the presence of a kingdom that has already been established by God. The kingdom of God and of redemption are interrelated. Repentance connects God's kingdom to us when we obey His commandments. Belief must be tied to repentance, because a person shows their belief by their actions. Faithfulness without action or "works" is dead. Another way of putting it is that "believing in something is mute when action is silent." When you believe in something, the evidence of your believing is the actions taken because of what is believed. Yeshua tells Israel to "repent" for the kingdom of heaven is near. He speaks in an imperative tone; it was not just a suggestion. The message entails a return to God's instruction. Repentance is to *change direction* or to *turn around*, beginning within one's own heart.

In the time of Yeshua, the Temple system was central to worship for Israel. Years of religious tradition had evolved. Israel's nationalism had focused on sacrifice, prayer and charity. As a nation alienated in their own land, all Israel had were men's interpretation of Torah. Socially, politically, and religiously, repentance was about "doing" as opposed to simply being the Lord's chosen. Remember that the Bible is a book written by the Hebrew people. The entire message of the Scripture is *repent*. In the context of Matthew 4:17, the message is *return, Israel, to walking in God's path*. Without repentance, there can be no redemption. Israel had to turn from sin and take action towards the Lord's commandments. True repentance is a heart and behavior issue. In the message of repentance, salvation is not personal; however, it is still a call to the individual.

> The Pharisees and the scribes asked Him, "Why do Your disciples not walk according to the tradition of the elders, but eat their bread with impure hands?" And He said to them, "Rightly did Isaiah prophesy of you hypocrites, as it is written: 'This people honors Me with

their lips, But their heart is far away from Me. But in vain do they worship Me, Teaching as doctrines the precepts of men.'" *Mark 7:5-7*

Regeneration connects to repentance based on what the Lord has already established. Repentance is the active participation of turning away from sin and walking in the ways of God. From the beginning, with Moses receiving the Torah and transmitting it to Israel until now, repentance has been the theme of the Bible as it has related to the nation of Israel.

In Judaism, there are generally four steps in turning towards the Lord:

1. Stop sinning.
2. Feel regret.
3. Confess to God.
4. Make a life change.

These four steps all involve an active change that establishes the Lord's covenant as the way of one's life.

> So you shall observe to do just as the Lord your God has commanded you; you shall not turn aside to the right or to the left. You shall walk in all the way which the Lord your God has commanded you, that you may live and that it may be well with you, and that you may

prolong your days in the land which you will possess. *Deuteronomy 5:32-33*

The ways of God bring glory to Him. In the context of Scripture, the call to repentance was not addressed to Gentile believers in the way Christianity has previously taught it. Repentance in the Bible was a national observation for Israel. Non-Jewish believers must first acknowledge this and recognize that the Lord's redemptive plan works throughout time and history. The theme of the Bible involves cycles of rebellion, exile and return to God. Old Testament prophets were notorious for their cry of return whenever Israel walked in idolatrous ways. When the prophets were ignored, Israel as a "nation" went into exile. The prophet's admonition was never a personal affair, although it would be an individual choice to heed or disregard the prophet's call of return. The Bible gives clear accounts of Israel's cycles of exile and restoration by the Lord's hand.

Repentance is about the full measure of God's standard: being separated unto the Lord. It is about living a life at a standard of holiness which is according to the Lord. The process of repentance began in the character of the Hebrew nation when Jacob's name was changed to Yisrael (see Genesis 35:9-12). "Yisra" in the Hebrew language means to be in a straight line, path or thought. It indicates *upright, remain, reserve and remnant.* The Hebrew word *el* is God. When looking at Jacob's name change, it is, in fact, a prophetic undertaking of repentance for his twelve sons, which later would become an entire nation with a mission to remain upright before the Lord.

Israel received the commandments and was responsible for living out the true nature of their ancestor's name and mission before the entire world. Israel was and remains a nation of kings and priests, living as the Lord's example of his kingdom. Through repentance, Israel's standard forms the example as to how to approach God in righteousness. Righteousness is not a doctrine or a legal term of acquittal. Righteousness is about a *justice experience* through obedience. Being declared righteous did not provide instant access into the Temple for worship. Nor was righteousness a revolving door whereby a person could do what they wanted one day and think forgiveness would come the next, upon presenting an appropriate offering. Biblical righteousness was rather a concept of the Lord's own character and concerns.

According to Habakkuk 2:4, the righteous live by their faithfulness. The first letter in the Hebrew word for righteous is "tzadi". It is the same first letter that is used to spell "tzelem", the Hebrew word for the image in which God created man. When the spirit man is born again, it is birthed in the unbroken image and likeness of the Holy One Himself. *Tzelem* relates to the levels of the soul: mind, heart, and action. Regeneration is the catalyst for the restoration of a person's soul.

> Jesus answered him, I assure you, most solemnly I tell you, that unless a person is born again (anew, from above), he cannot ever see (know, be acquainted with, and experience) the kingdom of God. *John 3:3 (AMP)*

Repentance is about a change of life that leads a person into a faithful relationship with the Lord. The righteousness of God means living faithfully as a holy people. Righteousness is *correctness* in Hebrew culture. Correctness is acceptability or uprightness. The upright are those that walk in the ways of the Lord. Righteousness is being on His path. For righteousness to be fully expressed, it is important to convey it from what we find in biblical culture.

Righteousness is justice. God's justice administrates what is honorable and true. Righteousness implies being created in the Lord's image and fulfilling one's moral responsibility. In the case of Israel, righteousness was embodied in the commandments within the covenant. If God was the initial King over Israel, then He expected moral integrity and truthfulness from His people. He expected Israel to pursue Him since He had demonstrated His faithfulness and loyalty consistently to Israel—even when they had turned away from their covenant with Him.

> Now then if you will indeed obey My voice and keep My covenant, then you shall be My

> own possession among all the peoples, for all the earth is Mine; and you shall be to a kingdom of priests and a holy nation.' These are the words that you shall speak to the sons of Israel. *Exodus 19:5-6*

> Then the Lord spoke to Moses, saying, Speak to all the congregation of the sons of Israel and say to them, 'You shall be holy, for I the Lord your God am holy. *Leviticus 19:1-2*

Israel is important in relation to the world; but the ultimate purpose for humanity goes beyond the history of a nation. Israel is a small, but very important, snapshot of a much larger picture in the whole scheme of God's plan for all of humanity. *Kingdom repentance* is about returning to the Creator where all things began. There is nothing within the context of time that supersedes the beginning, where God and Adam were one.

> Jesus spoke these things; and lifting up His eyes to heaven, He said, "Father, the hour has come; glorify Your Son, that the Son may glorify You, even as You gave Him authority over all flesh, that to all whom You have given Him, He may give eternal life. This is eternal life, that they may know You the only true

God, and Jesus Christ whom You have sent. I glorified You on the earth, having accomplished the work which You have given Me to do. Now, Father, glorify Me together with Yourself, with the glory which I had with You before the world was. *John 17:1-5*

In the narrative of John, Yeshua is praying a prayer of return prior to His death. Yeshua, as the living Word, functions as the "one who causes to save." Salvation is always a present act for the Hebraic mind. For Greek thinkers, salvation is seen as something in the future. Salvation is the unity of God's eternal will and word in the "now".

> Behold, God is my salvation, I will trust and not be afraid; For the Lord God is my strength and song, and He has become my salvation. *Isaiah 12:2*

> The Lord is my strength and song, and He has become my salvation. *Exodus 15:2*

Salvation is a present action. The biblical mindset focuses on the present, disregarding the future; while the Greek mindset focuses on the future, disregarding the present. The prayer of Yeshua is focused on the present but has eternal implications, which include the past, present and future.

Yeshua's act of obedience was, indeed, humanity's entire act for those that believe in him.

Repentance regenerates truth, because truth is the Lord's final reality of life. As living substance, truth is glory's revealing power. The domain of light is the territory of righteousness under the sovereignty of a King. Kingdom repentance is about knowing the Lord's greater truth; it is returning to the Holy One Himself.

In His Majesty's Presence

> He asked life of You, You gave it to him, length of days forever and ever. His glory is great through Your salvation, splendor and majesty You place upon him. For You make him most blessed forever; You make him joyful with gladness in Your presence. *Psalm 21:4-6*

Majesty is a supreme status. *Presence* is the state of existence or occurrence. Spiritually speaking, "in His Majesty's Presence" is a legal term which denotes and demands the utmost status and dignity and respect. Eternal life exists in and through the indwelling majestic presence of the Lord. Salvation joins a person to the substance of a holy glory. Glory is the garment worn by kings who serve as priests in the Eternal Father's court. Glory honors what is spoken in the courts of heaven—in the Lord's very presence. As it is in heaven (that is, in the Lord) so it is on earth (that is, in man from the dust).

Kingship reflects the process of maturity. Maturity is the experience of being responsible. Being spiritually responsible is responding to the Lord's wisdom. Godly wisdom is the ever-increasing power of insight into the things of God. When a person engages the Lord for the sake of the Lord's kingdom and not for vanity, all wisdom, knowledge and understanding becomes the way of serving. Wisdom, then, becomes the crown that rests upon the head of the Eternal King's servant. A person can only experience God through serving Him. Serving in the King's presence is an elevated position in the Lord. It is a place of constant awareness of the greatness of the Infinite One, Who passes all worlds and encompasses everything. It is the Lord that provides life to the created world, in a manner which permeates each recipient, according to individual capacity, as well as in a manner that transcends and embraces everything. Believers are to live through the eternal life of God by recognizing His greatness through the glory given to them as redeemed sons.

> What is man that You take thought of him, and the son of man that You care for him? Yet You have made him a little lower than God, and You crown him with glory and majesty! You make him to rule over the works of Your

hands; You have put all things under his feet.
Psalm 8:4-6

The Lord's thoughts towards man are majestic and glorious. His thoughts are full of honor and dignity. The Lord adorns man with a claim to an earthly and heavenly inheritance. When was the last time you went to your heavenly Father to ask for your inheritance from Him? Do you dare to think that way? In the book of Job, he speaks of being stripped of the Lord's glory and honor:

> He has walled up my way so that I cannot pass, and He has set darkness upon my paths. He has stripped me of my glory and taken the crown from my head. He has broken me down on every side, and I am gone; my hope has He pulled up like a tree. *Job 19:8-10 (AMP)*

Job's temporary position alludes to humanity's loss because of the "I". The restoration of wealth for the human soul and eternal spirit is the glory Yeshua speaks of in John 17. The richer one's perception of God's majesty, the greater will be his hunger for His Majesty, the King.

One's true preparation and direct path for repentance has to do with the release of self-glory in its entirety. Nothing can have glory in the King's presence except the King Himself. All self-glory is destroyed through a broken and contrite heart.

Living as a sacrifice is to actively participate in the breaking off of all forms of arrogance and pride.

> The sacrifices of God are a broken spirit;
> A broken and a contrite heart, O God,
> You will not despise.
> *Psalm 51:17*

The LORD is near to the brokenhearted and saves those who are crushed in spirit.
Psalm 34:18

For thus says the high and exalted One Who lives forever, whose name is Holy, "I dwell on a high and holy place, and also with the contrite and lowly of spirit In order to revive the spirit of the lowly and to revive the heart of the contrite." *Isaiah 57:15*

Being in the Lord's presence is a glorious experience. It can only happen with the shattering and removing of all carnal defilement. All false light coming through "self" must be destroyed when entering into the Lord's light. The light of Yeshua's glory reflects within the hearts of those who answer to His name. It is to function according to the nature of the Father's character. God is the only Creator of all creation seen and unseen. Yeshua, as the son, is the King that restores the Father's rule and order. Salvation administrates the sovereignty of the Father. Salvation never negotiates it. As Yeshua is resurrected in the fullness off his glory, so are all who believe that He is the Messiah, the begotten Son of God. This redemptive process includes all of creation. God has never lost control of anything: only the relationship with His steward, the "manking". On the simplest level, our perception of God in the world is through His actions. Every name by which we call Him reflects how we perceive Him. However, what is more important is how He calls and sees us.

> Now then, if you will indeed obey My voice and keep My covenant, then you shall be My own possession among all the peoples, for all the earth is Mine; and you shall be to Me a kingdom of priests and a holy nation.'
> *Exodus 19:5-6*

> But you are a chosen race, a royal priesthood, a holy nation, a people for God's own possession, so that you may proclaim the excellencies of Him who has called you out of darkness into His marvelous light; for you once were not a people, but now you are the people of God; you had not received mercy, but now you have received mercy. *1 Peter 2:9-10*

In the context of Scripture, it is clear here that God is speaking to the Israelites. But in the context of the Spirit, there is an invitation extended to the entire world. It is a royal estate that executes the Lord's sovereignty in the entire earth. This sovereignty is the dominion of the Infinite One, in the domain of people made in His image and after His likeness. The kingdom of the Infinite One is the kingdom of the Ancient of Days. The impression believers are to make in the world is to be faithful to God's ultimate omnipresence: His glory.

> Blessed be the LORD God, the God of Israel, Who alone works wonders. And blessed be His glorious name forever; and may the whole earth be filled with His glory. Amen, and Amen. *Psalm 72:18-20*

His Kingdom's Glory

The statements "His kingdom's glory" and "His glory" are not the same. God's true glory is difficult to comprehend in all its fullness; whereas the glory of His kingdom is everywhere. It is not difficult to experience the Lord's kingdom glory when one is living a submitted life, according to His will. A statement of faith is a declaration to the King that gives testimony to who He is. A testimony of faithfulness is the life lived out of a salvation that goes from glory to glory;

not story to story. Yeshua's obedience resulted in His kingship and it is evident by our sacrifice and His continued resurrecting power. The Lord is still reviving areas of our heart at all points of glory. When we are touched by the Lord's presence, it is His love that overtakes the darkness within our heart. The eyes of our heart gather more light in order to see better. There is a correction of seeing. His kingdom is the kingdom of everything, seen and unseen. True faithfulness is that which is stamped upon the soul by the Lord's light. Salvation speaks, "Let there be light." The secret of our eternal inheritance is sealed within the relationship that we are to have, as born-again believers through the begotten son, Yeshua.

> The Spirit Himself testifies with our spirit that we are children of God, and if children, heirs also, heirs of God and fellow heirs with Christ, if indeed we suffer with Him so that we may also be glorified with Him. For I consider that the sufferings of this present time are not worthy to be compared with the glory that is to be revealed to us. *Romans 8:16-18*

There is a revealing of the Father that is taking place now on the earth. This revealing is God's seal on creation. To be the seal of God is to live out of His truth. Knowing truth brings the freedom needed to express the will of the

King. Truth itself is the conclusion and culmination of all creation. In His glory is a *kingdom position of authority*. Serving for the sake of the King's majesty and glory creates an eternal standard for the world in which we live. It is an eternal standard because "The Lord shall reign forever and ever." (Exodus 15:18)

The reign of God is for always. The height of the Lord's Spirit, after all is said and done, is the "commanding" revelation of the infinite "treasure-house" in God's absolute glory. The inner sanctuary of a person's spirit is the living temple of God, in His beauty and splendor. Believers have the privilege to know the essence of God through the salvation given to them. Divine nature is perceived first through the service of our silence or "submission". Silence is where no worldly language corrupts the record of glory. It is the circumcision of the heart and tongue; the separation of good and evil that wants to communicate any form of self. In the Lord's kingdom glory, as sons of God, we must be joined to the Lord, for this is our ultimate level of divine service.

Take-away Thought

> But when the kindness of God our Savior and
> His love for mankind appeared, He saved us,
> not on the basis of deeds which we have done
> in righteousness, but according to His mercy,
> by the washing of regeneration and renewing

by the Holy Spirit, whom He poured out upon us richly through Jesus Christ our Savior.
Titus 3:4-6

Regeneration and glory are interconnected. The true purpose of this regenerated life is to develop a relationship with the Almighty King of glory. Regeneration is to be clothed with the honor of the revealed Messiah. In this honor, obedience is critical because it puts you in the correct position as a son. The spiritual pleasure we have as believers is the experience of the Father's love and the knowledge of His desire for us to be close to Him. When we draw close to the Lord, He will draw near to us. It is important to appreciate everyone and everything around you. Through appreciation, we find there is relationship with the Holy One Himself. Daily we can experience glory by honoring others in such a way that it brings them into a living reality of God's kingdom.

Regeneration reinstates divine order and godly alignment. Everything physical has a spiritual purpose. All that exists was set in place by a greater source in order to be valued and glorified for its God-given purpose. It is the Almighty that has determined purpose for all things by His design. How everything functions is a moment-by-moment reality in which everything is in process of reaching the Lord's eternal goal. People who are not regenerated spiritually cannot see the Lord's purpose in all things. The Master of the universe is very much aware of all things and is working all things out that still hinder His glory.

In the Lord's perfecting will, our limited intellect, our limited abilities and our limited memory are no match for the divine destiny set in motion for those called by the Lord's name. The Lord does not forget anything He has ever created and is constantly mindful of everything in creation. The Lord's ability never runs thin nor does it ever fall short. Yeshua destroyed all evil that works to destroy God's glory. By conquering our personal passions and concentrating on being stewards in creation, we become masters over all that opposes God. The eternal gift of God is life, His regenerated glory.

> And He who searches the hearts knows what the mind of the Spirit is, because He intercedes for the saints according to the will of God. And we know that God causes all things to work together for good to those who love God, to those who are called according to His purpose. For those whom He foreknew, He also predestined to become conformed to the image of His Son, so that He would be the firstborn among many brethren. *Romans 8:27-29*

Chapter 4

Control—Alt—Delete: The Renewed Mind

> If you really listened to him and were instructed about him, then you learned that since what is in Yeshua is truth, then, so far as your former way of life is concerned, you must strip off your old nature, because your old nature is thoroughly rotted by its deceptive desires; and you must let your spirits and minds keep being renewed, and clothe yourselves with the new nature created to be godly, which expresses itself in the righteousness and holiness that flow from the truth. *Ephesians 4:21-24 (CJB)*

New nature must be expressed by a reflective redemption. As it is in Yeshua, the King of Glory, so is it to be for those who are in him. Being birthed into the Lord's kingdom carries with it a great responsibility. Responsibility to the Lord is the result of a new nature and a transformed heart. Living in God's will begins within the heart of a person. The Lord still looks for the response to His initial call to mankind, "Where are you?"

> The kingdom of the world has become the kingdom of our Lord and of His Christ; and He will reign forever and ever. *Revelation 11:15*

The ruling power in the world can no longer be a legitimate answer because salvation has given the first and last answer to the eternal call of the Father. As Aleph (Alpha) and as Tav (Omega), Yeshua is the eternal memory of who was, who is and who is to come. Yeshua as the Word is the substance of the great "I AM", which makes true sons. We are sons through His glory reigning and remaining forever and ever. Believers have a privilege and a position that responds to, but should never react to the Lord's will. Yeshua never reacted to anything in His life. Throughout His lifetime on earth, Yeshua knew His Father's will and responded in obedience. It is because of Yeshua's obedience that there is salvation. The faithfulness of the Messiah demonstrated glory, honor and supernatural authority over all creation.

One who is carnal in nature reacts to life with a *control—alt—delete* mindset. In short, the *control—alt—delete* function is conceived so as to interrupt or enable an interruption on a computer. The *control—alt—delete* mindset constantly reboots the soul when it gets locked into an old memory which freezes the person in the same old, routine action. This mindset only resets itself and cannot be considered renewed.

As with computers, there is both hardware—that is, tangible technology—and there is software, or "intangible" technology. The human mind and body can be compared to hardware. It is the hard drive of a person that holds data, programs and viruses, etc. The mind and body encounter day-to-day life and, in doing so, hold the memory of it. The memory then becomes the software, by which the person will begin to live. Computer software tells a computer what to do. These instructions are core commands, such as updating the system clock or responding to external input received from the keyboard or mouse. Likewise, the mind stores life's memories, much like a graphic card (images), keeps a record of time (clock) and receives worldly influences (input). What is on the hard drive (i.e., mind) of a person cannot be erased but the mind can still be renewed to the original operating conditions through the mind of Messiah.

We live in a world where technology has made life quicker; and when things run faster, there is a greater likelihood of them crashing. Many believers fail to know the Lord's standard of glory because they experience only a "clean hard drive" spiritually. Once a person is born again, they attempt to wipe off all old data or old thoughts, old words, and old actions from their mind through their changed behavior. They go to church. They read their Bible. They "do" ministry yet they still struggle in their natural mind and body. These well-intended actions are not the process of sanctification. Sanctification means to experience a miracle greater than the freedom from the bondage of sin. Sanctification is to experience the revelation of God's light, and to express the honor due to Him by changing how we live. When looking at salvation from the position of sin, we see how it directs the eyes to see only through the nature of sin. Sin nature is the "software" and this nature is running on an operating system called the "self". The problem with this is that believers need to see salvation from the position of glory, not the position of sin. The King of glory operates from glory because sin no longer exists—it is actually destroyed. Ask yourself this question. *Are you operating from glory in the Lord's life?*

> For this reason also, God highly exalted Him, and bestowed on Him the name which is above every name, so that at the name of Jesus every knee will bow, of those who are in heaven and on earth and under the earth, and that every tongue will confess that Jesus Christ is Lord, to the glory of God the Father.
> *Philippians 2:9-11*

The action of erasing the "hard drive" of the mind is not enough because there is still an image there somewhere. For true glory to rest in and through a person, there must be a complete shift of everything, starting with the operating system. We cannot be simply wiped clean and then reload the new software called "religious works" on old hardware. When there is a new operating system software released, the hardware must be able to support it. For the Lord's standard of glory to occur on the earth, the Lord's perfect memory must be inserted into the spirit, soul and body of a person. Man is nothing more than God's memory chip. It is good to note what a memory chip is and how a memory chip is made.

My wife, Sarah, is an electrical engineer. She worked for Samsung at one point and was responsible for making memory. She shared with me how making memory was a delicate process of layering. Memory chips consist primarily of silicon, which is obtained from sand. The process of making sand into silicon involves melting, cutting, polishing and grinding. Then the silicon is pressed and cut into integrated circuits for use. Please note that this is not the complete process of how a memory chip is made. But did you notice the key ingredient in the memory chip? Yes, it's sand! Memory is sand.

> Then the Lord God formed man of dust from the ground, and breathed into his nostrils the breath of life; and man became a living being.
> *Genesis 2:7*

The dust of the ground received the breath of life and in that moment God released an eternal record and man became the Lord's "memory chip" in creation. Nothing else in creation carries this except man. The renewed mind is a mind that lives in the first revelation of life. It is to remain constant, according to the measure of glory released. There is no compromise, nor is there any complacency in glory. Compromise is to cooperate with darkness. It is like settling for what the enemy says, although what he speaks is not true. Complacency is to be satisfied in "self-rightness". Complacency carries with it haughtiness because it determines its own contentment. An unrenewed mind will conform to what is easiest and will do as little as possible whenever it can. An unrenewed mind will see and want the best of everything, but will give out the least possible sacrifice to obtain it.

There is a difference in what you allow in your identity and what you identify with. When we compromise, we give away our identity and, in doing so, we forget who we were in God. Man was contaminated through his disobedience and the impurity of sin damaged his memory, causing him to be blind to the eternal things of God. God's chip (man) lost what he once carried in glory. In the formation of man, the Lord placed an eternal recording that is to cause man to know glory. Man was pulled from the dust of the earth and this dust was in a glorious state. The ground was not cursed until after man's disobedience. The state of the dust before sin-nature had the capacity to become whatever holiness spoke. It was transparent and pure. To be pure is to see, because all things are revealed and nothing is hidden. When we see we will know what the Lord intends. This is because of man's reflective glory as God's image and likeness. Man is formed from holiness and is eternal spirit.

The Mind's Character

All character issues exist because of a compromise within the soul. Compromise creates the atmosphere for complacency. Regardless how difficult it may be to overcome, compromise and complacency require a "decentering" from self. Transformation begins and ends with the mind being renewed into a mind that is centered on the Lord. A mind that fails to be renewed will have intellectual flaws. Intellectual flaws come to know things through mistakes, failing and weaknesses. These flaws lack the wisdom of God; therefore they cannot receive or understand the mysteries or the treasures of heaven.

Another aspect of the unrenewed mind involves character flaws. When there is honor, the character of a person will reveal the nature and design of God. In such a person God's own kindness, love, joy, peace, patience, justice and mercy will be reproduced. Character flaws will devalue or exaggerate these and so destroy the true essence of a person.

> At the last it bites like a serpent; and stings like a viper. Your eyes will see strange things; and your mind will utter perverse things. *Proverbs 23:32-33*

When we take from what the Lord forbids, we are bitten in the end. The poison of the enemy causes the eyes to see strange things, and through the eyes the mind will speak perversion. In other words, the eyes are gates into the mind. And if left unguarded, the mind's eyes will mislead, mismanage, misinterpret and misstep. The carnal mind must undergo the Lord's renewal process.

> Therefore if there is any encouragement in Christ, if there is any consolation of love, if there is any fellowship of the Spirit, if any affection and compassion, make my joy complete by being of the same mind, maintaining the same love, united in spirit, intent on one purpose. Do nothing from selfishness or empty conceit, but with humility of mind regard one another as more important than yourselves. *Philippians 2:1-3*

Only the Lord can bring His mind into a person. However, we can put ourselves into position before the Lord so that we can receive His mind. Obedience prepares the mind. Obedience is earthly restoration to a divine manifestation. Rejecting temptation restores truth at the highest level in the mind. The more we obey, the better we are prepared. Preparation is critical to gaining the mind of Messiah, united through love, and having one purpose. This one purpose is to glorify the Father. It is to bring one's integrity and nobility into the Lord's will as one progressively obey Him. Obedience, as introduced previously, connects to humility. The Father resists the proud but gives grace to the humble. Having the same mind as the Messiah brings fellowship with the Spirit of God. This fellowship conveys a friendship and an active partnership.

A friendship with God can happen only when the mind's character is centered on honoring the Lord in all things. Glory is the only substance that can unite someone with God. We are partners with God through His mandate to us in Genesis 1:28 (i.e., to be fruitful, multiply, subdue and to have dominion). This mandate comes out of the kingdom of God in order to meet the needs of creation. The needs of creation will be met when a son of glory is revealed. As each level of glory transforms the mind, the reality of this walk with the Lord clothes the believer with humility. Yeshua was clothed in humility when he veiled his divinity and took on human flesh; this was his service. This is to happen for every believer, but it is in reverse sequence. Our humanity is veiled by the glory of the Lord's salvation. We take on the Lord's honor through humility. Humility is the highest level of glory for man. God is not looking for a perfect human. He is looking for humility that has perfected a person in order to reflect who He is.

> Then He took the five loaves and the two fish,
> and looking up to heaven, He blessed them,

and broke them, and kept giving them to the disciples to set before the people. And they all ate and were satisfied; and the broken pieces which they had left over were picked up, twelve baskets full. *Luke 9:16-17*

Why is feeding the multitude considered a miracle? Was it really a miracle? Or was it a demonstration of a son? Notice what Yeshua does. He blesses, and creation responds with fruitfulness and multiplying. There was a need and the fish from the sea came forth. The seed with fruit in it came forth in the wheat of the bread. Yeshua does just as he saw His Father doing at the time of creation. He blesses, just as God did in Genesis. And with His blessing, increase came. It was no miracle for someone who knew the Creator of all things. Yeshua, a son or "a steward tending to His Father's house (that is, creation)" was present; and there was, and still remains, a commensurate response from the creation.

I think it is interesting that there are twelve baskets left over. Could it be a prophetic meal that is still available? *Twelve* is considered a number for governmental rule. Was there an eternal government being re-established on the earth that was to demonstrate authority and power—the Lord's stewardship? I wonder if the twelve baskets full that were left over were for those like us who were not there physically; however, we were there at the original blessing mandate in Genesis 1. Do those baskets speak of a purpose for all who come to the King of King's table? The Lord's table has the King's portion, a portion where everything is full of grace and truth for a true son of the Most High.

Yeshua is clothed in humility before His glory is restored. He humbled Himself, taking on the form of a bond-servant. In taking on the power of death, Yeshua is highly exalted above all. When we live in the elevation of Yeshua's resurrection, glory will be our humility. Humility is where the natural ends and the supernatural begins. It is the disrobing of all humanity. Humanity is living now at the level of knowing good and evil. The carnal mind lives where flesh rules. The cross is the only way to deal with our carnal humanity. The cross puts to death the reality of all slavery, as well as the stripes within the flesh of slavery.

From Glory to Glory

> Now the Lord is the Spirit, and where the Spirit of the Lord is, there is liberty. But we all, with unveiled face, beholding as in a mirror the glory of the Lord, are being transformed into the same image from glory to glory, just as from the Lord, the Spirit. *2 Corinthians 3:17-18*

Evil seeks to be served, and the one way evil is served is through the mind. The Lord wants His will done on the earth. There are many missed opportunities because of the deception of the enemy. The greatest of these opportunities is the Lord's revealing glory. Liberty is the evidence of God's revealed glory. The freedom from all forms of "self" propels believers into extremely powerful places in the Spirit of God.

> You younger men, likewise, be subject to your elders; and all of you, clothe yourselves with humility toward one another, for God is opposed to the proud, but gives grace to the humble. Therefore humble yourselves under the mighty hand of God, that He may exalt you at the proper time, casting all your anxiety on Him, because He cares for you. *1 Peter 5:5-7*

The garment of the Lord is glory. The garment of humility is honor. The Lord is looking for a heart to rest in. When I say *rest* I am not referring to inactivity. I am referring to the Lord's Oneness. Yeshua's unity with His Father existed because of the authority that ruled him. Unity with God is an "interdependent" reality. Nothing in God is independent. All creation functions under the providence of God. The Lord's providence facilitates His glory.

> Blessed be the Lord God, the God of Israel, Who alone works wonders. And blessed be His glorious name forever; And may the

whole earth be filled with His glory. Amen, and Amen. *Psalm 72:18-20*

All life and blessings filter down from the Lord. Trust and confidence in the Lord removes worldly concessions and establishes the splendor of God's kingdom in creation. A person will experience the Lord only at the level at which He reveals Himself. At each level, there is increase of the Spirit. The increase of Spirit allows a greater measure of spiritual revelation. When glory comes into contact with a person, it does so to become a part of that person, because glory is eternal. Though the moment may pass, what remains is divinely eternal. This is the expansion of the Lord's kingdom glory. The Lord is always with us; however, when the Lord puts His hand on a person's life, He says emphatically that his time of corruption is over.

Yeshua explained how He and His Father were one. He tells His disciples that "if you have seen me, you have seen the Father." Everything Yeshua spoke and did came out of His place in His Father. Salvation is found when we are in the correct position so that we may hear the Lord's calling. Ignoring God's presence in creation removes the purpose of the creation because of His unity with creation. The more we are transformed into the image of a son, the less conformity to the world there will be in us. We release the control of thoughts to the grace of God whereby we are able to encounter the beauty of the Lord's holiness.

Going from glory to glory renews the mind and forces us to look at those areas in our lives that give place to the enemy. When worldly culture is filled with "wordy" values, people tend to think less of God. True sons of God can devote themselves only to what is real as born-again believers. And what is real is, in fact, the eternal glory that still engages the glory we had back in the beginning, before we lost what we had in God.

I often ask believers: "Are you seated in heavenly places?" Tell me what is your life like since you were born again, and your eyes were opened to eternity? Describe it if you can." The spiritual system that operates in the Lord goes from one level of glory to another. The world is purely physical to the unrenewed mind. For the person who is walking in the reality of God's love, there is an impressive capability revealed over all the power and the works of darkness.

Mankind is accountable and responsible for their thoughts and actions. After salvation is received, the mind must begin to focus on living in the truth of God's unwavering love and kindness. Because of Genesis 1, we know all creation is designed to respond to the will of God. This is the nature of creation including man. The nature of man is the Lord's glory itself, in all of His fullness. Every time we act in sinful nature, we are essentially saying that God's truth is not what is best for us at that moment. This mindset causes in us a separation into darkness, away from light. This kind of behavior indicates a person is not living at the level of the Lord's glory.

The spiritual laws that govern natural laws are wrapped up in the substance of the Creator's glory. The world was, is and will always be full of God. It will continue because He has placed all things into position to honor Him. By the function of God's great design, the mind of mankind reaches all the way back to what was in the beginning and remains until now. Good and evil contaminated holy perception. Now, in Yeshua, life is abundant and the believer sees as the Father gives sight to the renewed mind. The lie people live daily is the result of the loss of sight, because they fail to keep their minds renewed by salvation.

> Never lie to one another; because you have stripped away the old self, with its ways, and have put on the new self, which is continually being renewed in fuller and fuller knowledge, closer and closer to the image of its Creator. The new self allows no room for discriminating between Gentile and Jew, circumcised and uncircumcised, foreigner, savage, slave, free man; on the contrary, in all, the Messiah is everything. *Colossians 3:9-11 CJB*

Take-away Thought

> Consider it all joy, my brethren, when you encounter various trials, knowing that the

testing of your faith produces endurance. And let endurance have its perfect result, so that you may be perfect and complete, lacking in nothing. But if any of you lacks wisdom, let him ask of God, who gives to all generously and without reproach, and it will be given to him. But he must ask in faith without any doubting, for the one who doubts is like the surf of the sea, driven and tossed by the wind. For that man ought not to expect that he will receive anything from the Lord, being a double-minded man, unstable in all his ways. But the brother of humble circumstances is to glory in his high position. *James 1:2-9*

Humility partners with God and the reward is the ability to know God in all of His glory. It is a glory that pursues justice and truth. This righteousness implies that those who are created in the Lord's image must exercise righteousness in their daily lives. This righteousness is regarded as an eternal duty to the King of Glory. The duty of the renewed mind is to bond with the kingdom of God in all of its glory.

When the Lord reveals Himself, He also bonds with us. Bonding is an essential quality to endurance. When a person expresses an unwavering commitment to a person or experience, a bond is formed. There is a commitment, which comes through humility that is so great that a person will endure anything to preserve it. A relationship without bonding will not endure. The Lord's authority is the cornerstone of endurance. Endurance accepts the testimony of the King of glory through the human spirit. When we are humble, the best comes forth. The greatest example of this is Yeshua. And the greatest testimony to this is how we live out the Lord's salvation.

> [For being as he is] a man of two minds (hesitating, dubious, irresolute), [he is] unstable and unreliable and uncertain about everything [he thinks, feels, decides]. Let the brother in humble circumstances glory in his elevation [as a Christian, called to the true riches and to be an heir of God]. *James 1:8-10 (AMP)*

Endurance is the life of humility. As the mind is being renewed, correction comes. The correction of the mind causes focus and gives direction. Yeshua could only do what He saw His Father doing. What He knew was what He saw. What He knew was the result of His humility (in submission to His Father), not His humanity. Humility is the silent partner of endurance. As a man, Yeshua lived to honor His Father's will. In Yeshua's yielding, He acknowledged that His own life was for the glory of creation and the glory of His Father.

All the qualities and strengths that we have are not our own. They are given to us by God for a higher purpose—one greater than just the satisfying of our own needs. Endurance draws its power from the acknowledgement of humility. Athletes physically train for endurance, but it is the mind that will determine their victory. Their victory is because they see themselves in the place of honor, standing there in the winner's circle.

> Therefore, since we have so great a cloud of witnesses surrounding us, let us also lay aside every encumbrance and the sin which so easily entangles us, and let us run with endurance the race that is set before us, fixing our eyes on Yeshua, the author and perfecter of faith, who for the joy set before Him endured the cross, despising the shame, and has sat down at the right hand of the throne of God.
> *Hebrews 12:1-2*

Shame is to suffer being despised. It is important to come out of the agreement made with the false covering of an unrenewed mind. The renewed mind is a higher mind. It is a humbled mind that has the power to endure. As sons of God through Yeshua, we can see beyond human capacity. When a person surrenders before the Almighty, there is a transcendent experience into the glory of God. By this experience true humility provides the power for total objectivity.

True sons know what the Father is doing. They know His Spirit, His voice and His love. It is by the Lord's Spirit that we express His glory, and so we are given wisdom, compassion, discipline, endurance and, most importantly, humility. The Lord will not give His glory where pride resides. A platform must be created for the Holy Spirit in order to reveal what is already present within a person. Maturity of mind is to say, "I *do* know." Knowing brings us into the realm of the Lord's majesty and glory. It is what has been awakened in you—to know—because knowing has always been from the beginning. The natural mind does not comprehend this. What is with the Lord was in the beginning and, indeed, still remains and always will be. Understanding this is the renewal of the mind.

> Thus says God the LORD, Who created the heavens and stretched them out, Who spread out the earth and its offspring, Who gives breath to the people on it and spirit to those who walk in it. "I am the LORD, I have called You in righteousness, I will also hold You by the hand and watch over You, and I will appoint You as a covenant to the people, as a light to the nations, to open blind eyes, to bring out prisoners from the dungeon and those who dwell in darkness from the prison.

I am the LORD, that is My name; I will not give My glory to another, nor My praise to graven images. "Behold, the former things have come to pass, now I declare new things; Before they spring forth I proclaim them to you." *Isaiah 42:5-9*

Chapter 5

Dying to Live – The Living Sacrifice

For from Him and through Him and to Him are all things. To Him be the glory forever. Amen. Therefore I urge you, brethren, by the mercies of God, to present your bodies a living and holy sacrifice, acceptable to God, which is your spiritual service of worship. And do not be conformed to this world, but be transformed by the renewing of your mind, so that you may prove what the will of God is, that which is good and acceptable and perfect. For through the grace given to me I say to everyone among you not to think more highly of himself than he ought to think; but to think so as to have sound judgment, as God has allotted to each a measure of faith. For just as we have many members in one body and all the members do not have the same function, so we, who are many, are one body in Christ, and individually members one of another. *Romans 11:36 -12:5*

One of the most misunderstood principles in the Bible is the principle of sacrifice. Sacrifice traditionally implies loss or the giving up of something. The word sacrifice denotes an offering of something for a higher purpose. Sacrifice is the idea of propitiation or an act of worship. The sacrificial system of the Old Testament of the Bible is complex and filled with many types and reasons, all foreshadowing the Savior's sacrifice.

> Here is how God showed his love among us: God sent his only Son into the world, so that through him we might have life. Here is what love is: not that we have loved God, but that he loved us and sent his Son to be the kapparah for our sins. *1 John 4:9-10 (CJB)*

Yeshua is truly a living sacrifice for sin and guilt. The word "kapparah" is the Hebrew word for acquittal from sin, or for atonement. In Leviticus 16:30, God says "for it is on this day that atonement shall be made for you to cleanse you; you will be clean from all your sins before the Lord." Atonement is "kippur", involving expiation. Before going any further, I want to express the importance of the language.

The Hebrew language is purposeful and practical. It always indicates how a thing operates. Kippur has a root that means "to cover, cleanse, pardon, or purge". Kippur generally has two themes: acquittal and cleansing. Acquittal and purification are a direct response and resolve for the effects of sin. Kapparah is forgiveness or the withdrawal of claim. It is a legal concept. Kapparah, by function, says one may release a debt owed to him. When guilt is pardoned, then there is no need for penalty. Kapparah removes the need for punishment.

The Hebrew word for sacrifice is korban. This word has no implications of giving up something of value. Loss is not the emphasis of korban. Korban is related to the Hebrew word "karev", meaning "to be near". A korban was an offering through which a person sought to draw near to God. In ancient times, Israel would dedicate a perfect animal as a sacrificial offering and as a means of drawing closer to God. Their sacrifices did not provoke feelings of pain or regret over a diminished flock. The act of a sacrifice indicated gain because it implied something was being brought into the presence of God. A sacrifice was, and still is, to approach or come near to God; therefore there is never a sense of loss.

The purpose of the sacrifice was to bring friendship. In the temple structure, a sacrifice was to bring the sinful person closer to God because there had been a separation. The temple of Jerusalem, with all the priestly rituals, was for "ritual" purity. Transgression against God made the person impure or unfit, not able to engage God and His holiness. Celebratory meals always included the sacrifice of an animal. The "meat" would bring people together to celebrate good news or some joyous event. The sacrifices of the temple brought God and His people close.

The unfortunate interpretation of sacrifice as a loss misses the greater intent of God. Whatever comes into the Lord's presence is always increased. In salvation, Yeshua is an offering to atone for sin, which brings people closer the God. There is close friendship restored between God and man. This restoration is the attainment of a higher sphere of life—spiritually and physically, supernaturally and naturally.

The highest level of relating to God is obedience. God's highest level of relating to man is His faithfulness. Salvation is not getting "saved". Salvation is to step through the sacrifice of Yeshua and into the reality of where He is, now! Salvation is getting "covenanted". This reality is God's revealed work through the holiness of His Spirit. The Lord's holiness functions to reveal the majesty of all that is good. It is the separation leading us to fulfil the Father's will and purpose. Good is all that operates by the design of the Creator. Yeshua's sacrifice restores the "gravity of glory." Gravity of glory is the affluence and treasure that pulls towards us the significance, the impact, and the consequence of the Creator's success. God is very successful at all He does and His success was before anything was ever created.

> And the Word became flesh, and dwelt among
> us, and we saw His glory, glory as of the only

begotten from the Father, full of grace and truth. *John 1:14*

Yeshua is God's revealing glory in time, but it began in eternity. There is no failure in God. Therefore there is no failure in His salvation. Being born again should not be limited to a doctrine, whether old or new. The testament to God is His glory. The sacrifice of the Lamb of God removes the sins of the world. When sin is removed what remains is what was created.

Glory is the power to facilitate dominion. Dominion is not taking over. A king never takes over what is already theirs. Dominion governs. Glory governs by a directive substance between man and his Creator. This substance is salvation: "and the word became flesh." Man cannot tell his Creator what, how, when, why or where to create. Man is only able to return the sacrifice of his life by obeying the laws of nature that are of his Creator's design. This is not limited in any way, but is the ever flowing, increasing expansion of God Himself. Since all things come from within God, there is no place void of His glory.

Real salvation will always demonstrate obedience and faithfulness. Being a living sacrifice is not to lose your life but to bring your life into greater alignment, which is God's glory. The Lord will execute His reward or punishment for whatever comes into His presence. It is a standard not based on good or evil, but the Lord's glory and holiness administered in truth and righteousness. As a living sacrifice, God looks for the sacrifice of obedience.

Samuel said, "Has the Lord as much delight in burnt offerings and sacrifices as in obeying the voice of the Lord? Behold, to obey is better than sacrifice, And to heed than the fat of rams. "For rebellion is as the sin of divination, and insubordination is as iniquity and idolatry. Because you have rejected the word of the Lord, He has also rejected you from being king." Then Saul said to Samuel, "I have sinned; I have indeed transgressed the command of the Lord and your words, because I feared the people and listened to their voice. Now therefore, please pardon my sin and return with me, that I may worship the Lord." But Samuel said to Saul, "I will not return with you; for you have rejected the word of the Lord, and the Lord has rejected you from being king over Israel." As Samuel turned to go, Saul seized the edge of his robe, and it tore. So Samuel said to him, "The Lord has torn the kingdom of Israel from you today and has given it to your neighbor, who is better than you. Also the Glory of Israel will not lie or change His mind; for He is not a man that He should change His mind." *I Samuel 15:22-29*

Saul lost his place as king because of his disobedience. Samuel says "For rebellion is as the sin of divination, and insubordination is as iniquity and idolatry. Because you have rejected the word of the Lord, He has also rejected you from being king." Samuel speaks of something hidden within Saul's disobedience. When the Lord instructs a person to do something, obedience is a living sacrifice to the Lord. When a person disobeys, the life of that person becomes the sacrifice to whatever is obeyed that is not the Lord. What Samuel is actually saying is "obedience is better than becoming the sacrifice."

Being a living sacrifice is always centered on obedience and remaining faithful. Obedience is the active movement of love and devotion towards the things of God. Faithfulness is the active response of a disciplined heart towards God's will. Together obedience and faithfulness produce life. Life is the standard of the Lord's glory, releasing kindness.

Disobedience disqualifies a person from being a living sacrifice. Disobedience is the fruit of iniquity and is the substance of rebellion. Rebelling against God brings loss and failure, making it the sacrifice to the kingdom in darkness. Darkness prevents the glory of God because there is no light or revelation. An impure heart is corrupt and cannot experience the Lord. Saul thought his idea of worship was better than what God had commanded. When we think our ideas are better than God's, then we lose sight of any and all form of worship we can offer.

Worship, in biblical culture, was about being obedient. This is why the sacrifice and obedience are interconnected. They reveal where a person's heart truly is and whether God can call upon the person to respond to His glory through obedience. Worship is not a song; it is service—a response to the Lord. Being a living sacrifice includes always coming into the Lord's presence.

Behavior testifies to the existence of God in a person's life. The fact that God exists does not make Him "your God." The Lord is only your God when you relate to Him as a man or woman, created in His image and after His likeness. It is not just about words spoken but about actions taken to express the Lord's glory. It is not enough to declare your faith or have a belief; it requires living a godly life that demonstrates the glory of God through His authority. True belief compels us to live by the standards of the Lord.

Man determines the depth of his relationship with God based on his choice, which is the first *operating system* of man. And this system has crashed. God's glory draws a person into an intimate relationship, where he will become the sacrifice in which the glory will reside. I am not referring to a "woe is me" attitude or suffering for the sake of the gospel. Most people are suffering not for the sake of the gospel but for the sake of the "gossip". God desires to dwell where *love*, His greatest command, is building a dwelling for Him and His glory. God's kingship depends on our yearning for relationship with the Father. We become His sons when we accept salvation's sovereignty. As a living sacrifice, we must have a resolve with divine intention concerning the Father's heart and household. Yeshua's kingdom requires the willingness to accept governmental rule.

> For a child will be born to us, a son will be given to us; And the government will rest on His shoulders; And His name will be called Wonderful Counselor, Mighty God, Eternal Father, Prince of Peace. There will be no end to the increase of His government or of peace, On the throne of David and over his kingdom, To establish it and to uphold it with justice and righteousness From then on and forevermore. The zeal of the Lord of hosts will accomplish this. *Isaiah 9:6-7*

The proclamation of Yeshua's sacrifice announced a kingdom of justice and righteousness. Yeshua willingly allowed the government of the world, with all its worldliness, to be placed on His shoulders. In doing so, the increase came to His Father's kingdom. To be a living sacrifice, we must be willing to see increase beyond ourselves. In Yeshua's kingdom His glory is in His exalted position as King of Kings and Lord of Lords, but also in the glory of those joined to Him to serve as kings and lords over the Father's estate—the earth and all it contains.

It is human nature to resist leaders that control instead nurture by virtue. Corruption, abuse and the misuse of leaders' power will cause rebellion. Presenting yourself as a living sacrifice is the final act to see God's glory. It is transformative and unchangeable. Sacrifice is coming closer to God. And the closer you get to God, the greater the weight of His glory will rest upon you, causing His standard to be known and seen. John the Baptist said "He must increase, but I must decrease." (John 3:30) John was laying down his life for the sake of the Savior that had come into the world. John saw the greater glory when he looked upon Yeshua. "Behold, the Lamb of God who takes away the sin of the world!" was John's cry. He testified to the living sacrifice that would bring the world close to God. Though John decreased, it did not mean that he thought less of himself. Thinking less of ourselves makes us unworthy of the blessing. Thinking more of ourselves is equally bad. The substance and the vessel must be the same. Yeshua was in His Father and also in His disciples. Yeshua was joined to His Father in a spiritual union with a physical outcome.

In Hebraic thinking culture people are never without God. Everything is dependent upon something else caused by God. Loving God requires obedience. Obedience breaks off the old selfish nature in order to bring the Father's will into our lives and into the world around us. Love for God is a supernatural response. Love for each other is the extension of this supernatural response, making us *super natured*. I call it "super natured" because the transformation of the heart changes the nature of the person. In this transformation, there is a spiritual shift that translates us into the Lord's eternal destiny. To go from glory to glory is a standard for spiritual action. All spiritual actions involve facing the Lord. When facing the Lord, there are five things that serve as reminders for being a living sacrifice. These are:

1. Righteousness: character and concerns of God
2. Justice: administration and execution of God's will
3. Loving-kindness: saving acts of God
4. Compassion: generosity of God
5. Faith: willingness of God

The key to the Lord's purpose is His providence. Providence is divine as it relates to salvation. It allows God's wisdom, insight, perception and provision to direct a person's path. It is because of righteousness that the Lord orders the steps of man to live out his life with a holy awareness. Having an awareness of the Lord's presence acknowledges His closeness to us and our closeness to Him. When walking at this level of holiness with God, it is easy to separate what is done in selfishness and what is done in His image and after His likeness.

The Father wants to bring all those that are willing and able into His glorious presence for His sake and His kingdom's sake. Believers are accepted in the beloved and by the beloved. Four actions can be taken to live in the beloved. These are:

1. Learn: taking on the yoke of Yeshua, "His commands and His ways."
2. Teach: share the reality of Yeshua's yoke
3. Guard: fortify the heart against all corruption
4. Do: remain faithful to the will through obedience

Yeshua's yoke is not used to suggest a burden. It is used in the sense that the animal has no idea of what its master's will is. The animal is in absolute submission. The yoke is the means of enabling the animal to fulfill its functions. Every born again person must realize that their faithfulness is based upon the Lord revealing Himself. The purpose for this revealing is for the glory of the Lord throughout all creation, bringing forth God's eternal will and purposes. Our Father wants us to return all things according to His glory. As sons, our responsibility is to tend to the Father's business. Creation is our Father's business and His children are the household stewards.

Take Away Thought

A living sacrifice is the Lord's drawing us close. Many people never become a true living sacrifice for the Lord. A living sacrifice is based on maturity of spirit. Immaturity disqualifies a person because immaturity is self-seeking and often prideful. Immaturity prevents the experience of the Lord's glory and power. Glory is based on integrity and morality within the context of daily living. It is a blessing to fulfill the Father's will as a son; it brings honor to Him.

> He who offers a sacrifice of thanksgiving honors Me; And to him who orders his way aright I shall show the salvation of God.
> *Psalm 50:23*

The beauty of a soul is without distractions. I've coined the phrase "a distraction is a demonic attraction." It is what interrupts the flow of the Father's will and purpose in the earth. When life is lived at a superficial level, inner glory goes unnoticed. It is vital to direct our eyes and heart towards God in salvation. When our eyes and heart are centered on the Lord, then we participate in holiness, as set apart believers. We are in the Lord and therefore not of this world. We live in the restorative process as an image and likeness of God, reflecting the King's will as living sons. We must want to be emptied of all carnality because it rejects the presence of God. The Lord Himself wants to reveal His love and strength; and obedience facilitates this. When we obey the Father's will, it makes His presence greater in the earth, and this is His strength as the Creator and ruler in those that are His sons.

The greatest challenge in living as the Lord's sacrifice is humility. The Lord resists the proud but gives power to the humble. Living as a sacrifice is not a life of suffering. It is a life of awe and splendor before the Lord. There may be some suffering for what has yet to die in the flesh. But a sacrifice that goes through the cross finishes in a place of power and authority. The High Priest of Israel wore the most beautiful clothes when he stood ministering before the Lord. The priests were able to partake of the best portions of the offerings. They lived before the Lord in humility, although they had the best of the land. The difference was in how they saw their position as servants before God. It was the heart that had to remain pure and low. In their heart they always had to remember that serving in such an exalted position was due to the Lord's sovereignty and nothing more.

> Then Jesus said to His disciples, "If anyone wishes to come after Me, he must deny himself, and take up his cross and follow Me. For whoever wishes to save his life will lose it; but whoever loses his life for My sake will find it.
> *Matthew 11:24-25*

Living as the Lord's sacrifice is chastening. Our Father loves it when we say no to ourselves. In denying self, what remains is what has gone through His chastening. Humility must be disciplined and focused. Humility is yielding. Being humble recognizes and acknowledges that the capacity to endure and prevail, with no compromise, is not from self. Yeshua humbled himself and, in doing so, He became the greatest expression of glory. His humility built something lasting. The giving of His life is the testimony that He was the Father's Son.

The function of Yeshua's name serves as the living sacrifice that causes the experience of the Lord's glory and the majesty of His kingdom. As joint heirs with the Messiah, we share in this spiritual responsibility to God's glory. Loving God and doing what He asks of us are interconnected. True love leads to action. If actions do not follow, then love is questionable at best. Our allegiance to the kingdom is revealed when the Lord's glory crowns us. As it is in the Lord, so it is to be on the earth. To clarify, I will shift to the tabernacle of Moses referenced in Hebrews.

> Now the main point in what has been said is this: we have such a high priest, who has taken His seat at the right hand of the throne of the Majesty in the heavens, a minister in the sanctuary and in the true tabernacle, which the Lord pitched, not man. For every high priest is appointed to offer both gifts and sacrifices; so it is necessary that this high priest also have something to offer. Now if He were on earth, He would not be a priest at all, since there are those who offer the gifts according to the Law; who serve a copy and shadow of the heavenly things, just as Moses was warned by God when he was about to erect

the tabernacle; for, "See," He says, "that you make all things according to the pattern which was shown you on the mountain." But now He has obtained a more excellent ministry, by as much as He is also the mediator of a better covenant, which has been enacted on better promises. *Hebrews 8:1-6*

See that you make them after the pattern for them, which was shown to you on the mountain. *Exodus 25:40*

In his ascent, Moses sees, in the heavenly realm, the Lord's dwelling place. God commanded Moses to make Him a sanctuary, showing him what it was to be like. Moses was allowed to see the pattern of the things in heaven that God also needed on earth. It was to be built after the pattern of heaven. What is God's is eternal. To say that the eternal pattern has been done away with because of the earthly pattern is wrong because time cannot erase eternity. If time cannot erase eternity, then what Moses was able to see and accomplish by the Lord's grace remains. Better does not mean what was before is done away with. *Better* here speaks of how something is accomplished. The standard for Israel's glory was in the centrality of worship in the tabernacle, and later the temple. The standard of glory now is in the tabernacle of man's heart, erected by Yeshua. The eternal pattern of the original blueprint of man is his image and likeness of God. God is the architect of this blueprint. Yeshua, in all of His revealed glory, is the pattern within the blueprint. God's Word has always been and will never pass away. Believers must ask, then, what is salvation as it was, is and always will be? What, then, is the standard that we are to live by? What is gained by the death and resurrection of Yeshua that is eternal right now, at this time? How does the Lord dwell in His kingdom among His people? What is the yoke of heaven for believers?

> Let your light shine before men in such a way that they may see your good works, and glorify your Father who is in heaven. *Matthew 5:16*

Believers in the salvation of Yeshua are to demonstrate the covenant of God and His sovereignty. Salvation is acknowledging the Lord of the universe in both the seen and the unseen. Glory proclaims the honor of God. The Lord's standard to live by must be established within a person for glory to be discovered. As righteousness becomes the standard of God's pervasive army in the earth, uncompromised glory is revealed. Our complete and absolute love must be greater than anything we possess, including our very life. Salvation cannot be negotiated for the sake of a "selfish life" or culture. Yeshua, as the eternal word, brings us into an eternal relationship with absolute resignation. There is no relationship with the Lord without the resignation of self. Let us look at Matthew 16 through the Amplified version of the Bible.

> Then Jesus said to His disciples, If anyone desires to be My disciple, let him deny himself [disregard, lose sight of, and forget himself and his own interests] and take up his cross and follow Me [cleave steadfastly to Me, conform wholly to My example in living and, if need be, in dying, also]. For whoever is bent on saving his [temporal] life [his comfort and security here] shall lose it [eternal life]; and whoever loses his life [his comfort and security here] for My sake shall find it [life everlasting]. For what will it profit a man if he gains the whole world and forfeits his life [his blessed life in the kingdom of God]? Or what would a man give as an exchange for his [blessed] life [in the kingdom of God]?
> *Matthew 16:24-26 (AMP)*

In my reflective moments before the Eternal King, I found that glory is in God's unconditional love. Even in the midst of what I had once thought to be good, the Lord opened my spirit to His revelatory breath and allowed me to know that there is no condition where He would not act on His behalf; this was His unconditional love for me. When the Lord reveals himself, His glory comes into contact with every part of our being and what is revealed becomes a part of us. The revelation does not leave us. The Lord's presence remains; He takes up residence in what was once our lost self. Regardless of what we believe, something is imparted and transforms us, whether we are aware of it or not.

Every person born on the earth comes from God with a fulfilled destiny that is eternal. That destiny is revealed in the spiritual identity that comes from God. No one is born without a purpose that did not begin in God, the Creator of all things.

This book is my attempt to shed light on the yoke of heaven and the concept of obedience in the Lord's household. Like the apostle Paul, everything we think we understand and know must be considered as dung. What we take on is important to God. If it were not, then returning to His glory would be for nothing. David, the son of Jesse, prays a simple yet powerfully prayer in Psalm 72. David says, "Blessed be the Lord God, the God of Israel, Who alone works wonders. And blessed be His glorious name forever; And may the whole earth be filled with His glory. Amen, and Amen." (Psalm 72:18-20)

Glory is heaven's benchmark breaking through time. God's love for His creation is tremendous and cannot be denied. The kingdom of God exists to make the King's will known. Salvation is to know and live the King's will. Salvation is the pathway by which victory is established.

God's people are not meant to just survive doing what is right. In the Messiah believers are righteously judged vessels of light that live as the standard of God's glory on the earth. As it is in Him, so it is now in those that are called by the name of the Lord.

I wrote this book for the purpose of getting back to basics. Foundations are important because they determine the quality of stability. If the foundation is solid, then it will uphold whatever is built upon it. Foundations are often disregarded because they are unseen. Foundations go unnoticed and, in some cases, they are given a lesser place. I wanted to write about what is most important—the Lord's standard of glory—because it is a foundation for salvation. Salvation must remain centered on the Creator, the Giver of life and light. My hope is to restore, if not renew, the hearts and minds of people by provoking them to stand with their shoulders square and their compass true. My prayer is for the reader to look with eyes and heart wide open to God's love. Allow the Lord's unveiling. Go where many will not go. Examine salvation in light of the Lord's glory and not personal insight. There are no theological debates when it comes to the heart. It is a matter of love and righteousness. A year ago my rabbi gave me a pearl of wisdom that I have since tried to incorporate into in my life. "You must know when to be right and when to be wise." Salvation is not being right; it is the Lord's wisdom expressed through His glory. Glory expressed is eternal life. Life eternal was, is and will always be.

What is man that You take thought of him, And the son of man that You care for him? Yet You have made him a little lower than God, And You crown him with glory and majesty! You make him to rule over the works of Your hands; You have put all things under his feet.
Psalm 8:4-6

Chapter 6

We His People

> "For my thoughts are not your thoughts, and your ways are not my ways," says Adonai. "As high as the sky is above the earth are my ways higher than your ways, and my thoughts than your thoughts. For just as rain and snow fall from the sky and do not return there, but water the earth, causing it to bud and produce, giving seed to the sower and bread to the eater." *Isaiah 55:8-10 (CJB)*

The Lord's standard is different from ours. Our human thinking is nothing compared to the Majesty of the Creator. The closest thing we have in knowing the greatness of God is His salvation that comes through the begotten Son Yeshua, the Messiah. Salvation expresses the image of the Lord's glory in all His fullness. This fullness is worthy of honor and praise to the glorified Messiah, Yeshua. He is the way to knowing the love and kindness of our heavenly Father. Mankind is God's image on the earth. This image is kingship, which expresses dominion and authority. Creation is looking for the image and likeness of its Creator. There is nothing anyone can do or say, other than what has already been done and said in and through God's will. Anything other than what the Lord has designed, and what salvation has fulfilled according to that design, is vanity.

The kingdom of God is the governmental rule of the spirit, soul and body purchased by the Lamb of God. A government is a system by which a people are governed. All governments must have laws to maintain stability. Government is comprised of administrators and officials whose responsibility is to make effective policies for the good of the people. When national policies are created, then the rules affect every aspect of human activity.

> What then if you see the Son of Man ascending to where He was before? It is the Spirit who gives life; the flesh profits nothing; the words that I have spoken to you are spirit and are life. *John 6:62-63*

God's law is His Word. God's Word sets in motion His will in all domains. God is Spirit and to serve Him requires spiritual knowing in order to engage the kingdom of God. The natural mind cannot perceive spiritual laws. However, there are examples of God's rules and how His people are to live under His rule. One example is Israel and the Torah. To understand this, *sovereignty* and *kingship* must be examined. Sovereignty and kingship are not synonymous.

Sovereignty is a dominion power with authority and control. It is independent, is subject to no one and is supreme over everything. Sovereignty carries the freedom to execute a will. Kingship is a sovereignty but it is dependent on the will of others. Kingship has limited control, based on territory. As it relates to God, His sovereignty is universal. Because God is the Creator of everything and everyone, His sovereignty is unconditional, and there are no options for creation. What is created is because God willed it so. Regardless of a person's way of life, everyone is accountable and will be made accountable to how they lived. Life comes from somewhere and life will return to the giver of that life.

> For the wrath of God is revealed from heaven against all ungodliness and unrighteousness of men who suppress the truth in unrighteousness, because that which is known about God is evident within them; for God made it evident to them. For since the creation of the world His invisible attributes, His eternal power and divine nature, have been clearly seen, being understood through what has been made, so that they are without excuse.

> For even though they knew God, they did not honor Him as God or give thanks, but they became futile in their speculations, and their foolish heart was darkened. Professing to be wise, they became fools, and exchanged the glory of the incorruptible God for an image in the form of corruptible man and of birds and four-footed animals and crawling creatures.
> *Romans 1:18-23*

Unlike sovereignty, kingship is determined by choice. A king is limited to a people or territory and can only sovereignly rule based on the will of a people. A good biblical example of this is the nation of Israel. The people of Israel were specifically chosen by God to be His kingdom on the earth.

> For you are a holy people to the Lord your God, and the Lord has chosen you to be a people for His own possession out of all the peoples who are on the face of the earth.
> *Deuteronomy 14:2-3*

The Lord chose a people through a covenant—in His sovereignty. Israel came into agreement with God's sovereign choice—His Kingship. Although God rules all creation, His specific government is seen in His people, Israel.

> ...Now then, if you will indeed obey My voice and keep My covenant, then you shall be My own possession among all the peoples, for all the earth is Mine; and you shall be to Me a kingdom of priests and a holy nation.' These are the words that you shall speak to the sons of Israel." So Moses came and called the elders of the people, and set before them all these words which the Lord had commanded him. All the people answered together and said, "All that the Lord has spoken we will do!" And Moses brought back the words of the people to the Lord. *Exodus 19:5-8*

Israel accepted God as ruler and agreed to do all that was commanded. Israel's *yes* established God's kingship over them as a specific kingdom with the Torah as the rule of government. This government ruled through a submitted will. "We will do" was Israel's response to the conditions that were later given at Mt. Sinai, and this made the eternal kingdom an earthly kingdom.

We must remember that the Torah (the instructions or the law of Moses) was not given as a way of salvation. Israel had already been delivered from bondage, so their freedom was in effect. The Torah served to show that the former slaves of Egypt were now free to live as sons, under God's rule, through the instructions given. The principles of sovereignty and kingship are in the Lord's salvation. The will of God was executed through the obedience of the son, Yeshua. The kingship of Yeshua continues to execute the Father's will within His body (the Church) through His sons of salvation. The willingness to obey the full counsel of the Father's Word establishes a nation of people. It is through our willingness that God's glorious kingdom prevails.

As believers, we mature as the governing body throughout creation. The Lord administrates His kingdom through the process of maturing His sons to become lords, then establishing them as kings. Yeshua is King of Kings and Lord of Lords. Accepting His kingdom gives us the honor of being joint heir in His lordship, as stewards of His salvation in our daily lives. In our faithfulness and obedience we become kings and "rulers" over creations, according to the Father's will on the earth.

> Now there was a man of the Pharisees, named Nicodemus, a ruler of the Jews; this man came to Jesus by night and said to Him, "Rabbi, we know that You have come from God as a teacher; for no one can do these signs that You do unless God is with him." Jesus answered and said to him, "Truly, truly, I say to you, unless one is born again he cannot see the kingdom of God." *John 3:1-3*

Being born again is our entrance into the kingdom of God. Yeshua has a conversation with Nicodemus expressing the need for rebuilding God's government among the people. The faith of the Jewish people had diminished for what the Father had intended for His people. The elders of Israel had made their relationship with God based on the doctrines of men. Scriptures were taught through interpretation, leading to tradition. Israel's spiritual leaders had become blind guides, leading the people of God into yokes that burden God's people. The whole temple structure and all the religious works needed to be changed and rebuilt in order to free men from the theology of the day.

To be "born again" meant to become like a child—to learn everything anew. It was to have all thought, attitude and habits changed. When a child is born it knows no hate and has nothing in its heart against anything or anyone. Born again literally means "born from the head. Think about it, a child comes into the world headfirst: It is called "crowning". Being born again is regeneration. Yeshua is saying "start over." Imagine Nicodemus, a scholarly man of great reputation, being told to get rid of what he has accomplished. All our accolades, awards and honors don't get us into God's kingdom. Unless we become like children, none of us can enter into the Lord's kingdom. Yeshua knew that justice and love built God's kingdom. The kingdom of justice, built by God's love, is in the heart of His sons who are seeking to build the Father's house on earth.

> The Jews then said to Him, "What sign do You show us as your authority for doing these things?" Jesus answered them, "Destroy this temple, and in three days I will raise it up."
> *John 2:18-19*

When foreigners would invade Israel, their wealth and treasures would be taken away as part of the spoils of war. This included what was in the temple. When the temple was attacked, it was an attack on the priesthood. Yeshua, living in a Roman occupied land, understood the importance of creating a pure place of worship, where no enemy could steal the true riches of God—man's spirit and soul. The sovereignty and kingship of Yeshua rest in the people who know that serving begins with spirit, and with the truth of that spirit. God created an intangible and tangible socio-economic kingdom where the riches of heaven and the reality of earth are restored to the beauty of holiness and the brilliance of the King who rules what is both visible and invisible.

In God's economy, He removes the debt of sin that caused the sting of death. Through the debt removal, we have victory over the grave. All who accept the faithfulness of Yeshua are able to, once again, engage the Father as a son. The Lord's government operates by the law of God's unconditional love and His government carries no debt. Yeshua's death and resurrection cleared all of humanity's debt that was caused by sin, iniquity and transgression. Think about that!

All debt—past, present and future—is non-existent in God's kingdom. Everything caused by debt has been destroyed and should not have power in the kingdom of God.

Many people are in debt today because of an undisciplined lifestyle. The need for instant gratification is self-centered. The enemy is able to keep people captive because of carnal desires which will lead to some form of debt, whether physical or spiritual. Again! THERE IS NO DEBT IN GOD'S KINGDOM. Why are there so many believers in debt in what is considered the kingdom of God? Why is it harder for people to live at the level of a lender and easier to live at the level of a borrower? How can believers live in God's freedom when they are bound to the debt system of the world? When there is debt, people are not able to give properly to God due to the "enslavement" that debt creates. In truth, there is no credit given to a slave; only years of serving. Debt is a liability that obligates a person to serve it.

Debt is based on compulsive desires. Debt of any kind destroys the exchange of the eternal and patience for the temporary and instant. The Lord instructs us, as His sons, to owe no man anything, except love. Why? Because love is the active participation of always bringing honor to the Father's house.

Most governments carry huge amounts of debt to run them. This debt is paid for by the people of that country, through taxes collected from the people. All nations throughout the world operate on some type of system where debt is involved and a currency is used for commerce exchange. In the Lord's kingdom there is no debt and the currency is forgiveness. Forgiveness serves as currency because it removes debt. The true economic system within the kingdom of God runs by forgiveness not money.

> [In fact] under the Law almost everything is purified by means of blood, and without the shedding of blood there is neither release from sin and its guilt nor the remission of the due and merited punishment for sins. *Hebrews 9:22 (AMP)*

Forgiveness is the pardon of God because of His compassion. All that is done in God's kingdom is due to what He excuses and covers with His mercy. Being born again is the spiritual encounter with the Lord's saving acts that express His love for us. Mercy covers the effects of what sin causes. In the Holy of Holies of the temple there was no grace seat, but there was a mercy seat that covered the ark. Mercy is when the Lord covers the debt or penalty of sin with His own blood, giving access to God. Forgiveness is the exchange rate of God's kingdom and this exchange is maintained by love.

The greatest command is to love the Lord our God with everything we have been given. As God's people, we have been given the power to be what we were created to be for the Father as His children. It is by the blood of the Lord that we overcome the world and this blood is the exchange of love that clears the way to the Lord's glory. Yeshua's blood is poured out on the cross, covering sinful flesh, and the record of His blood spoke out between heaven and earth. Yeshua actually gives a command: "Father, forgive them" as the judgment against all works of darkness and thus He frees man from ALL debt. The once corrupted soul is cleansed and the spirit is free to live by the rule of love, in the law of God's spirit.

Being born again makes us the people of God. The transfer from darkness to light allows us to know the substance of infinite revelation that expands the administration of God's kingdom. Yeshua is not only God's sovereignty in the earth but He is also God's kingship. It is by the living Spirit that we live, move and have being through salvation. In this salvation God's word begins to separate spirit from soul, and bone from marrow, in order to bring unity with the Father. Yeshua and the Word are the same and cannot be seen as separate. God and His Word are the same. Salvation is the unbroken word or "substance of blood"—the life of the creature. You cannot see blood only as the red substance that flows through your body; it goes much deeper than that. You must seek to know what life is still applying the communion of Yeshua's blood.

Before Adam disobeyed the Lord, his soul was the "blood" to the spirit. Man becomes a living soul because of the life that the soul was given. The natural mind may not understand this, but if you seek the Lord He will show you what is being said here. Try not to use natural reasoning: It will not work.

The soul's redemption is the life given to the spirit. Salvation reclaims mankind by clearing debt through redemption. Salvation reclaims man's kinship with God through Yeshua.

To know the importance of kinship, we must look at the law of a kinsman redeemer. There were several reasons for the law of a kinsman redeemer. The most commonly known reason was the obligation of a kinsman as a married man's brother. According to the Torah, if a man died without leaving his wife a son, it was the duty of the deceased man's nearest male relative (usually a brother) to marry the dead man's wife and raise a son by her in the dead man's name. This was known as a kinsman redeemer and the purpose of the kinsman redeemer was to keep the deceased man's family going on the earth through the offspring which, in turn, maintained the family's inheritance. It was considered to be a curse to have one's name cease to exist, since that was part of the punishment for those found guilty of sins and who were "cut off" from among Israel. If, for some reason, the dead brother or the surviving widow had sold the family's property, it was the obligation of the living brother to buy back the property as well as to protect the wife. If the brother refused to fulfill his duty, it was considered to be dishonorable, and he would have to relinquish all ownership rights to the inheritance of the deceased kin that he would have received had he married his dead brother's wife.

A kinsman had several obligations for redeeming the next of kin. All of the reasons for the redemption were connected to a family's inheritance — land allotted to them by

God. The kinsman was of the same tribe and family and knew the importance of "keeping it all in the family." Maintaining family was critical for Israel. Family served as the house of God that demonstrated the Lord's faithfulness and power.

> And I heard a loud voice from the throne, saying, "Behold, the tabernacle of God is among men, and He will dwell among them, and they shall be His people, and God Himself will be among them. *Revelation 21:3*

The picture is much bigger when it comes to Yeshua being the kinsman that redeems. When Yeshua gave His life, an inheritance was restored. I briefly mentioned the kinsman redeemer but did not talk about the relevancy of it to salvation. Yeshua is considered our kinsman redeemer but this comes with mixed interpretations. Yeshua is the Lamb that takes away the sins of the world, but when looking at the laws of redeeming a kinsman, a man would never give up his life freely. How could a brother marry his widowed sister-in-law and die at the same time? How could the death of the person redeem a dead relative? Well it doesn't. A kinsman would never give his own life for the sake of gaining anything. It is true that Yeshua is the offering for sin on the cross, but He is also the Passover lamb of the Lord's table. While Yeshua is the Savior of the world, He is also the redeeming kinsman. A kinsman was a person from the same family, the same tribe and the same bloodline. When we look at Yeshua, we must ask how are we the same and how does He redeem mankind? How do the spiritual and the natural come together?

Adam is formed from the dust of the ground in Genesis 2:7. God breathes and man becomes a living being. This living being was the same as Yeshua. You must not only believe in the history of creation; you must know the history of creation. Adam was formed and God's breath of life quickened him. The Holy Spirit conceived Yeshua and He became flesh. Yeshua is our kinsman because we are from the same source— God. Yeshua purchased man's soul and restored our being to life. We are kin to Yeshua through the same Spirit that gave Him life at His resurrection. Just as we died by Adam's disobedience, we now live by Yeshua's obedience. Yeshua's redeeming power joins us to the Father and we live in Him.

> Because we know that Christ (the Anointed One), being once raised from the dead, will never die again; death no longer has power over Him. For by the death He died, He died to sin [ending His relation to it] once for all; and the life that He lives, He is living to God [in unbroken fellowship with Him]. Even so consider yourselves also dead to sin and your relation to it broken, but alive to God [living in unbroken fellowship with Him] in Christ Jesus. *Romans 6:9-11 (AMP)*

Take Away Thought

We, His people, now have the duty to continue the work of Yeshua by returning the family's inheritance to the Father. What is the family's inheritance? Creation! Believers are the next of kin as living spiritual beings. But this life is Yeshua's because it is He who is the kinsman redeemer. Not only does Yeshua pay the debt of sin that made man a slave, but He also returns man to the place of stewarding what belongs to the Father: All of CREATION! We, His people, are the government of God on the earth. We are spiritual beings, born anew. Our position before God comes through the King of Kings and Lord of Lords, and it just so happens that He is our next of kin. The blood of Yeshua is our lifeline to the Father and it determines who we really are on the earth. The blood restores both the spiritual and natural inheritance. Creation will respond when the true sons of God are in place according to the Lord's order.

Salvation is the Lord's redeemed glory. The redemptive blood of Yeshua restores the glory of God's truth. Yeshua is "eternal blood" or "eternal life." We have been given the capacity to engage God through the resurrected life of Yeshua. There is an unseen government waiting to be revealed inside every believer. How a person accepts salvation determines the level of God's glory that he will know on the earth. The message of repentance is the only gospel there is. Repentance is to turn towards our Creator and reflect what He is doing in

His redeemed kingdom. Just as Yeshua saw what His Father was doing, so can we who are the kingdom of heaven.

> To the praise of the glory of His grace, which He freely bestowed on us in the Beloved. In Him we have redemption through His blood, the forgiveness of our trespasses, according to the riches of His grace which He lavished on us. In all wisdom and insight. *Ephesians 1:6-8*

Chapter 7

Live the Experience

"They will not labor in vain, Or bear children for calamity; For they are the offspring of those blessed by the LORD, And their descendants with them. It will also come to pass that before they call, I will answer; and while they are still speaking, I will hear. The wolf and the lamb will graze together, and the lion will eat straw like the ox; and dust will be the serpent's food. They will do no evil or harm in all My holy mountain," says the LORD. *Isaiah 65:23-25*

There is a culture within a spoken language. All words, regardless of language, are known and heard by God. They are already purposed, even in the imperfections of language. The Word of God is understood at the level at which a language is known. When we interpret the Word of God through the language we speak, we risk taking it out of biblical context. The danger of doing this is that we will come to know God through the filters of how we know the language we understand. These filters are characterized by the culture we live in.

There is more to gain when the filters of understanding and assumptions are removed. All things are from God. And all things existed before our way of life and thinking was developed. Salvation through Yeshua means living by the breath of the Spirit. It means moving towards something, and that something is glory. And if we are living and moving by the Spirit, then we are eternal.

> I glorified You on the earth, having accomplished the work which You have given Me to do. Now, Father, glorify Me together with Yourself, with the glory which I had with You before the world was. *John 17:4-5*

The prayer that Yeshua is speaking is full and rich, bursting with supernatural opportunity. It is the Lord's real prayer. Yeshua's prayer is the culmination of His Father's will, beginning with the restoration of glory. I think sometimes believers miss this.

As Yeshua's mission in the dimension of His time on earth was ending, His language focusses on the eternal. His prayer is a clue to what happens when a person prays. When the soul and body are in the Lord's position, words change. What is spoken enter into a non-earthly realm because of God's will. What enters heaven is received and is returned from the Father changed; it is not the same language. We just don't recognize this because, unconsciously, we keep what has happened in earthly language form. The Lord's glory must clearly be seen in the lives of believers. Salvation is more than a confession; it is the experience of the Messiah's fullness. The begotten One lives as a Son, demonstrating His Father's love for creation. Glory was Yeshua's place of honor, above creation, as Lord and King.

> Just as the Son of Man came not to be waited on but to serve, and to give His life as a ransom for many [the price paid to set them free]. *Matthew 20:28 (AMP)*

We must realize that Yeshua came to serve and not to be served. The Father's will was fulfilled when Yeshua gave His life in service to accomplish what was needed. The restoration of God's glory was needed in the only living reflection of Himself that had been created; that is man (male and female). Yeshua came to serve and continues to serve through those who confess who He is throughout creation. Salvation is the experience of honor that brings glory to the Creator of all things. Born again believers carry the seed of righteousness, which brings the character of God and fulfills the concerns of God. Salvation is only concerned with the Father's will. Yeshua did this so much that it was the life substance of His being. Glory is about who believers are as servant sons. Yeshua wants us to be as He was in the beginning, before the world existed. It is a place of love and honor.

Love is the single most powerful and necessary element in life. Love is the origin and foundation of all human interactions. It is both giving and receiving. It allows us to reach above and beyond ourselves. Love brings the experience of another person to us and allows that person to experience us. It is the means by which we learn to experience the highest reality of God. Because of its power, love is the utmost. Every person's heart has the capacity to love. The question is whether it is actualized and how it is expressed.

For glory to become the standard, love must be the groundwork. You must ask the right questions of yourself: What is my capacity to love another person? Do I have problems with showing it? Does my love allow room for someone else? Do I suppress expressing love out of fear of reaction? Do I only love those that I relate well to and who relate well to me? Healthy love should always include discipline because it must be tempered and directed properly by the Spirit of God. If love is not properly disciplined through God's chastening, others may take advantage of us. This will hinder the Lord's glory. It is necessary to love with discretion to avoid giving to those who don't deserve it. When we love, our actions are honorable.

Honor is the other position of the glory. Honor is the principle of integrity in a person's life. I use the word principle because honor, at this level, is distinct and reverential. It is the kind of honor that withstands challenges and setbacks; the ups and downs of life. It stands ready to fight for the love you have for life and the giver of life. When honor is present, there is valor. Fear is not an option because love has perfected it.

Now ask yourself these questions: "Do I live in the certainty of the Father's presence? Does that certainty bring His truth on the earth?" Do I honor Him when I see myself? Is He honored in how I see others? Have I spoken unfavorably towards myself? Have I spoken unfavorably about others? Have I become a "garbage can" by listening to someone else's harmful conversation? As vessels of light and love, we carry holy things that cannot be mixed with an ungodly lifestyle.

Love and honor are two key necessities when it comes to the Lord's standard of glory that we are to live in. Mature love comes with—and develops—personal dignity. Honor comes from an intimate feeling of graciousness and mediation. Knowing your place and contributions in this world make you unique and remarkable. Any love that is debilitating and breaks the human spirit is no love at all and provides no honor. For love to be complete, it must have a measure of personal sanctification. Yeshua speaks of sanctifying us in truth. The Lord is looking for true worshippers who worship Him with spirit and with truth. Worship engages the destiny of who you are to become through the glory of the Lord's Spirit. You must know this in order to experience the Father spiritually.

There are three domains to be examined in order to understand how we experience God: Conception; Birthday and being Born Again.

Conception is the announcement. It is the beginning of the returning to God. When a child is conceived, it is God telling the world a return has started.

Birthday is the beginning of the record of return in time. It is how long it takes to return to God. But we cannot put this time period into eternity. When a person is physically birthed, it is the redeeming of something that was once in God and He wants that back. It is important to remember that we were all in Adam, and when Adam made a poor choice, divine intention was lost for a season.

Being born again is to enter into another realm of living. It is God's Word and our *yes* reawakened. It is Spirit life. The religion of the church offers a process when, in fact, being born again is memory. It is the memory of an eternal destiny through a spiritual life force. The Life force is the Lord's Holy Spirit being in control. Yeshua lived by the will of the Father. "Not my will but your will be done," is the decree of the King. In this divine decree is the authority, honor and glory.

When we are sanctified through spiritual worship, the sin of the flesh is being removed. Worship as it is in the supernatural should be imitated in the natural. It engages our entire being. The Holy Spirit transforms our lowly self into the image of a beloved son. Heaven opens up and God is well pleased. When we live, move and have our being in Him, it is because we are engaging the breath of God, and by His Spirit wind we are taken into His presence.

Our King desires that we know Him in the fullness of His glory. All affections and desires must function by the Lord's justice system, beginning with our salvation through Yeshua. Salvation is the way and should not be seen as a final destination. The final reality is to accomplish the Lord's will in and through all creation.

> Jesus said to him, "I am the way, and the truth, and the life; no one comes to the Father but through Me. If you had known Me, you would have known My Father also; from now on you know Him, and have seen Him." *John 14:6-7*

When a child is born it enters into the world at a specific date, time and place. In most cases, there will be a birth certificate, stating who they are by given name, as well as where and when they were born. The birth certificate establishes the child's citizenship of a country and, from that point on, that country becomes the government over that child. This governing body plays a key role in the development of the child, starting with the parents. There are expectations placed on the child as it grows into the "image" of what the parents have imparted throughout the child's life. Parents teach the child, within their culture, what is right or good, and what is wrong or evil in hopes of raising a responsible member of society. This brief description of birth can vary from person to person, but you get my point. The child was born into a place and lived accordingly.

> ...whose end is destruction, whose god is their appetite, and whose glory is in their shame, who set their minds on earthly things. For our citizenship is in heaven, from which also we eagerly wait for a Savior, the Lord Jesus Christ; who will transform the body of our humble state into conformity with the body of His glory, by the exertion of the power that He has even to subject all things to Himself.
> *Philippians 3:19-21*

Before salvation mankind's glory is the shame of desire, which is based on pleasing the self. Glory after salvation is the exertion of power and making all things subject to the Lord's perfecting will. With this in mind, I often ask born again people, "What does it look like?" Tell me, what and where are you in the Lord, having been born again? What does the delivery room look like? Who is with you, smiling and ready to give you the best of everything for you, in order for you to be a responsible member of the new kingdom?

Live the Experience

There is a citizenship for every believer in the Messiah. The residency of the Holy Spirit transforms our lives into the Son's glory by His glory and this causes all things to become subject to the King of Kings and Lord of Lords. Everything in heaven, on earth and under the earth must bow and give way to the standard of God's glory. As ambassadors of light, we are here to show others the way back to where all things were. Being sons of God makes us subjects of salvation. When the unredeemed world looks at God's kingdom, we must ask, "Does it see God?" Our lives must reflect where we are in the Lord. This is revealed by how the Father's truth shows in and through our lives. Worship facilitates this. Worship involves submission, and the only way to submit is through obedience. Obedience brings God's order into every situation and this is our worship.

Submission to God's will is to surrender all desires to His kingdom. Through surrendering, we relinquish the natural culture, including social norms that have governed our lives. Salvation is to engage the Lord, not the enemy. Remember that Yeshua, as Lord, overcame the world. The kingdoms of this world are now the kingdoms of His lordship. Allowing true lordship begins with our obedience, just as He was obedient. Obedience allows the glory and power of the resurrection to penetrate all darkness. Being rescued from the domain of darkness is being transferred into a kingdom where all things are laid bare. Nothing is hidden, not even in the DNA of man. There is no shame. There is no blame. There is no fear. One of funniest things that can happen to a person living in shame is that they blame. A person who lives blaming others is living in fear. And a fearful person is really a prideful person because of how they see things.

When pride is ruling, then a demonic principle is ruling. The Lord's salvation is the administration of being born again. The new birth destroys the glory of shame and clothes the person with the glory of grace and truth. The greatest experience is salvation. God's miracle was and will always remain His loving kindness towards us. It is His love for us that make His salvation so powerful. To ask for the experience of God's Spirit is to seek His salvation. The power of salvation is revealed through the Messiah.

Our spirit man encounters Yeshua at the place of His kingship and lordship. Yeshua is no longer a "suffering servant". He is the risen Son made alive in the glory that He had before the world was created. This is our standard — our starting point. The Lord continues to serve as ruler over all creation. Respect and awe will disciple all those who are called to salvation as they live out every day of their redeemed lives. True worship takes place when we acknowledge the salvation that sanctifies us to know the truth of who the Lord is. This is a direct encounter with glory, which then raises the standard of the Lord over our lives as born again sons of righteousness.

> This is the message we have heard from Him
> and announce to you, that God is Light, and

in Him there is no darkness at all. If we say that we have fellowship with Him and yet walk in the darkness, we lie and do not practice the truth; but if we walk in the Light as He Himself is in the Light, we have fellowship with one another, and the blood of Jesus His Son cleanses us from all sin. If we say that we have no sin, we are deceiving ourselves and the truth is not in us. If we confess our sins, He is faithful and righteous to forgive us our sins and to cleanse us from all unrighteousness. If we say that we have not sinned, we make Him a liar and His word is not in us. *1 John 1:5-10*

Take Away Thought

When our heart is in the correct position, our worship becomes about the Lord, in the fullness of His glory. As the Lord sees, so will we see. In his prayer in John 17, Yeshua says, "The glory which You have given Me I have given to them, that they may be one, just as We are one; I in them and You in Me, that they may be perfected in unity, so that the world may know that You sent Me, and loved them, even as You have loved Me." (verses 22-23) Salvation is the union of soul and spirit at the highest degree of love.

Love is the greatest experience of God's glory. Our response to God's selfless act of love is the complete acceptance of this love. Many people fail to know the Father's love because love, or the lack thereof, is viewed through a human experience. The average person will love based on what gives them pleasure. There are some people that love based on a need for security. This kind of love is from the "self" and it will always be concerned with the "I", "Me and "My". In truth, there is only one kind of love that is addressed by Yeshua when He is praying. It is the love that is elevated above the natural good and seeks the supernatural truth of God. It is a love that gives up life for the beloved. It is a love that clings to God in everything, at all times.

> You shall fear the Lord your God; you shall serve Him and cling to Him, and you shall swear by His name. He is your praise and He is your God, who has done these great and awesome things for you which your eyes have seen. Your fathers went down to Egypt seventy persons in all, and now the Lord your God has made you as numerous as the stars of heaven. *Deuteronomy 10:20-22*

The phrase *cling to* is not used much anymore, but it is one of the best verbs we have to describe the Lord's commitment to us and to His creation. Clinging is one of the first principles of God for mankind. Male and female were made to cling to each other. There is a law that operates in people because of this principle. God's natural law of reproduction is because of clinging. Clinging brings the increase of life. Without reproduction between male and female, the human spirit would not endure. The essential element of clinging is enduring. Enduring yields out of the strength of ones love for another. Yielding does not mean to lose one's identity but to accept the truth in the beauty of another.

To cling to God is the humble recognition and acknowledgement that the capacity to endure and prevail comes from the soul that He gave each person. It is in clinging that humility does not compromise because of the divine nature of the soul. God's love is demonstrated through Yeshua's humility when He endured the cross. Yeshua's prayer of glory and love sanctifies everyone who believes they are in Him, not just who knows about Him. Belief in the begotten Son requires meekness. Meekness is not weakness. Meekness is the silence of everything. There are no sounds other than the Spirit wind of the day resting inside the spirit of a person. Meekness involves absolute reverence towards the Lord and towards all who serve in His kingdom.

Living by the Lord's standard of glory requires that we be intentional in serving. We celebrate God's image and likeness in every person. We should never just tolerate or be tolerated, but always celebrate others. Tolerating people should never be confused with tolerating their behavior. On the contrary, loving people includes wanting them to be the best they can be and therefore helping them to be aware of anything less than perfect behavior. Living under God's kingdom standard of glory requires that we recognize our personal discipline as an expression of love. It includes the understanding that we have no right to judge others; we have a right only to love them and that implies wanting them to be their best. Ask yourself: When I judge and criticize others, is it, in any way, marked with any of my own displeasure and frustration? Is there any hidden satisfaction in the other person's failure? Or is it only out of love for the other person? If you see people from any other viewpoint other than God's, then you are seeing through the brokenness of your own soul.

The Lord's standard of glory for us is raised according to God's image and likeness. As sons of the Most High God, we are elevated to that position to serve. The Lord's way becomes our way of life. Our life is then glorified, bringing honor to our Father. Believers should bolster the best in a person, cultivating the Lord's sovereignty. We must, above all else, seek to express compassion in new ways that go beyond our previous limitations. The Lord's kingdom is advancing in power, might and glory and this is the true standard of His salvation.

We become that which we worship.
Saul Avila, Pastor Christ Community Center

For from Him and through Him and to Him are all things. To Him be the glory forever. Amen. *Romans 11:36*

Bibliography

New American Standard Bible – www.Bible Gateway
Complete Jewish Bible – www.Bible Gateway
The Amplified Bible – www.Bible Gateway
The Empty Chair – Rebbe Nachman of Breslov
Breaking the Serpent Code – Jim and Faith Chosa
www.thelivingwords.ancient-hebrew.org – "Unity" Jeff Benner
www.ancient-hebrew.org - Jeff Benner

CPSIA information can be obtained at www.ICGtesting.com
Printed in the USA
LVOW06s2347240915

455636LV00001B/3/P